FINDING YOUR JOY SPOT

FINDING YOUR JOY SPOT
Copyright © 2021 by Leona deVinne

Author: Leona deVinne

Cover design by: Fetching Finn

Published by: Our Family Lines

Print ISBN: 978-0-9917075-8-4

CONTENTS

Introduction

Your circumstances don't need to change for you to experience more joy.

I've encountered joy and seen overwhelming joy in the most unexpected places.

This book will help you find joy where you least expect it.

Won't that be great?!

To be honest I never gave much thought to joy until I started coaching clients.

As they started to understand themselves better and they had more clarity about the direction they wanted to move in there was joy-EVERY TIME!

The closer they got to what mattered to them, joy met them with a big smooch. It was amazing to be a part of that.

Joy gave them more energy, clarity, engagement, creativity, and direction in their lives.

The closer they got to the spots that were filled with joy, those joy spots were like a boost for their lives and businesses.

These joy spots were like a lighted landing strip in what might have otherwise seemed like a dark night. When they followed their joy, they knew the direction to move in, in order to find more meaning and purpose, and even more joy resulted.

The more they paid attention to their joy, the more they thrived and became even more successful.

At the same time, I was coming out of what was the darkest season of my life, as my 19-year marriage unravelled. It was devastating. What was more surprising was that as I moved through the pain, I felt more intense joy than I had ever known. There were spots of joy seemingly waiting to be uncovered. I might not ever have known had I not struggled so intensely.

This book is a compilation of blogs and my thoughts that I captured as I discovered more about joy. It is ultimately meant to be all about you finding greater joy as you discover more about yourself and what really matters to you.

Joy can seem to be hiding, elusive; perhaps you can't even remember the last time you experienced pure, blissful joy. Maybe every day feels dull. Same busyness, same pressure. Same. Same.

Maybe you can't remember the last time you felt its precious spark or felt its igniting goodness.

I know. I've been there.

I would ask, "Is this what life is supposed to be like?"

Here's the deal and the promise I make to you in the pages of this book.

Your life does not have to be perfect to experience exquisite, life changing joy.

Joy comes from the inside of you and this book will give you the guidance and the prompts that I've used with my clients to create more capacity for joy. And then I'll show you how to cultivate even more of it. Yum!

You'll become a joy gardener. ;)

You'll be digging up your truth and discovering your own joy spots along the way.

Wee little places that joy has been all along and now you'll get a chance to see their delicious goodness.

AND… shockingly this book is also steeped in science.

My junior high science teacher would probably drop dead knowing that I have become a science junkie. I was a very resistant and vocal student about how I hated science in school.

However, I can't get enough of truth and science. I don't want you to think this joy won't stick around. When it's birthed in the truth of what we know about joy and the truth about you-that's like joy glue.

I have filled this book with research-based knowledge that translates into skills to increase your well-being, resilience, happiness, and lets you flourish.

That's joy!

You'll be more aware, happier, healthier and JOY FULL. I promise. My life and my clients' lives have been transformed by doing the work in this book.

We get more joy when we seek it, we also get more when we look at some challenging places in our lives, those gritty bits, that require us to be brave and move through those areas to create more space for joy spots to show up.

Sometimes you read a book and enjoy it and maybe it evokes some change. This book is meant to be so much more. It contains stories, resources, techniques, and reflection exercises that will help transform your life.

It's the most incredible experience to have walked alongside someone as they're exploring something in their business or their life, and poof, seemingly out of nowhere, joy would appear as they uncovered more of what deeply mattered to them. That's what this book will do for you.

This book uses the tools I have used with my clients in order to help you discover more of who you are AND, as that happens, you will notice spots of joy show up and blow you away with its full out goodness. Like an unexpected kiss. So good.

I have taken situations from my own life to show you how joy is possible, even when things are tough. I give you the opportunity to create the change we all ache for and discover more joy than anyone could have anticipated.

This book will fill your life with new possibilities and new joy spots. Doesn't that sound delicious?

If at any time you want even more joy, stop by my website for some joyful gifts and, even better, set up a 20-minute complimentary session here: www.findingyourjoyspot.com. I so look forward to connecting!

How to Use This Book

Yes, this book does come with instructions. Think of them as your joy spot finding manual.

Some prep:

I recommend reading a chapter a day and taking the time to write and reflect on the subject of the chapter. This book can be read through like a novel, but you won't get nearly the impact for which it was intended.

Ideally, take some time at the beginning of your day to read and reflect on the content of the chapter for the best results. Think of this as your ideal joy spot finding prescription.

Each chapter will include a reflection section. Take the time to be with the questions and write down or think about the first thing that comes to mind when you answer the question. That's your intuition. You need that. That's where joy is birthed.

Some tools and questions will be repeated on occasion, that's so you know that these techniques apply to many situations and the questions might be similar. This is done to help you dig deeper and have a deeper understanding of you.

You will also need self care. Always. Think about how you can create space every day for you-time. Yes you. You need to be your top priority otherwise, everything else suffers. Maybe that's 10 minutes with a cup of coffee in the morning. Maybe that's a 20 minute walk by yourself, maybe a bath. You need time to nurture you. You're like the soil in the garden and if you're going to cultivate joy, you need some lovely "soil" in your life. A self care practice does that.

I work with people like you. From time-to-time, I'll remind you that you can reach out for support. Either way, I'm here for you. I have many complimentary coaching sessions to help you get out of the grind and get your groove on! Reach out and grab some joy giving goodies at www.findingyourjoyspot.com.

You'll also notice a letter at the start of every chapter. This corresponds to PERMA, five aspects of flourishing identified by Dr. Martin Seligman. Dr. Seligman is known as the founder of Positive Psychology and has been studying the *must have*s for well-being and flourishing for over 40 years.

The acronym stands for:

P - Positive Emotion

E - Engagement

R - Relationships

M - Meaning

A - Achievement

The science of PERMA is going on in the background of what you're going to encounter in this book. (Can you hear my science teacher passing out and hitting the ground?) If you read the chapters and then answer the questions after each section, you'll digest the information more effectively. We integrate information by writing. It helps a lot.

Take the time to answer the reflection prompts. Go with the first thing that pops into your head. Journaling is EXCEPTIONALLY good for you and is very transformational. (There's lots of science behind this goodness as well.) If that's not a pool you're willing to dive into, consider taking the questions and talking about your answers with someone, or take a question or two and think about them over the course of your day.

First, let's unpack PERMA a wee bit so you can see the secret sauce behind the sections of the book.

P – Positive Emotion

This element has perhaps the most obvious connection to happiness. Focusing on positive emotions is more than smiling; it is the ability to remain optimistic and view one's past, present, and future from an open-minded perspective.

A positive view can help in relationships and help to inspire others to be more creative and take more chances. In all of our lives, we have highs and lows; focusing on "the lows" does increase our chances of experiencing lower moods overall. We will look at some tough situations, but with the plan to move through them to find positive emotions, like joy, on the other side.

Regardless, there are many health benefits to optimism and positivity, which you'll discover while going through the book.

When a child completes building a complex Lego car that requires their concentration, for example, they might beam with joy and satisfaction from their work.

This type of positive emotion is crucial to increasing overall well-being. It can help people enjoy the daily tasks in their lives and persevere with challenges they will face by remaining optimistic about the outcomes.

E – Engagement

Activities that meet our need for engagement flood the body with positive neurotransmitters and hormones that elevate one's sense of well-being. This engagement helps us remain present, as well as synthesizes the activities where we find calm, focus, and joy.

People find enjoyment in different things whether it's playing an instrument, engaging in sports, dancing, hobbies or working on an interesting project. When time truly "flies by" during the activity, it is likely because the people involved were experiencing engagement.

We all need something in our lives that absorbs us into the current moment, creating a "flow" of blissful immersion in a task or activity. This type of flow of engagement stretches our intelligence, skills, and emotional capabilities.

R – Relationships

Relationships and social connections are crucial to meaningful lives.

Too often, the pursuit of happiness has this Western bias of "individuality" where each person steers their personal happiness ship to shore. This is not realistic. We are social animals who are hard-wired to bond and depend on other humans. Hence, the basic need for healthy relationships.

We thrive on connections that promote love, intimacy, and a strong emotional and physical interaction with other humans. Positive relationships with one's parents, siblings, peers, coworkers, and friends are key ingredients to overall joy. Strong relationships also provide support in difficult times that require resilience.

Basically, our pain centres become activated when we are at risk of isolation. From an evolutionary perspective, isolation was the worst thing we could do for survival because it meant that we would be cut off from other people and our chances of being fed and protected from danger were vastly decreased.

These activation centres are like fire alarms in the body, discouraging people from continuing to feel this pain, and ideally, towards reconnecting socially with someone, or a group. We need, neurologically, to know that we belong to a group; it helps us feel safe and valued and has for millions of years.

M – Meaning

Having an answer as to "why are we on this earth?" is a key ingredient that can drive us towards fulfillment. Meaning doesn't need to come from religion and spirituality. Working for a good company, raising children, volunteering for a greater cause, and expressing ourselves creatively can also hold meaning.

Unfortunately, the media worships glamour and the pursuit of material wealth, impacting many people to feel like money is the gateway to happiness. While we do need money to pay for basic needs, once those basic needs are met and financial stress is not an issue, money is not what provides people with happiness.

Understanding the impact of your work and why you choose to "show up at the office" may help you enjoy the tasks and become more satisfied with what you do.

A – Accomplishments

Having goals and ambition in life can help us achieve things that can give us a sense of accomplishment. You should set realistic goals that you know you can meet. Once you've reached the goals, you'll be filled with a sense of satisfaction, pride, and fulfillment.

Having accomplishments in life is important to push ourselves to thrive and flourish.

In addition to all the science that shows us how to flourish, it's important to know that you're here for a reason. I don't mean simply to read this book right now. I mean you were put on this planet for a reason.

You aren't like the other sevenish billion humans that currently inhabit our world.

You are you. Precious; precisely made to be you.

And I want to tell you a secret. Get a little closer.

You were made for something special. Maybe you forgot what it was. Maybe you left it behind in some previous chapter of your life.

Perhaps you've never felt its deep delicious embrace or that feeling of it gurgling up in your throat.

It's what makes you alive and makes life soooo worth living.

It's joy and joy is what you get when you live your truth.

It's a compass to find our way back to ourselves.

Want more joy?

Be more you.

If the thought of who you are, or of not even knowing who you are, makes you feel longing, or loss, or confusion, or even pissed off, then you're in the right place.

This book is your book. Your journey back to yourself.

It's a journey to joy and also a journey to you.

If you wouldn't know joy if it smacked you in the face, or if it kissed you fully on the lips, then I'm over the moon delighted that you're here. This is a book that will help you write your book-your book of joy.

Before we cheapen this wee three-letter word, I want to be clear.

This is not some watered down, how to be happy all the time, plan.

Joy is about you and your truth. You can feel joy when life is going your way and most importantly, you can experience the deepest joy in the darkest moments. It serves as our mainsail on the high seas and keeps us on track during the storms that life can bring.

It anchors us to the shores of our being and gives us the keenest sense of direction so we can move towards it and fill our days with purpose and meaning and with the wildest riches of what success brings. A wee FYI, that's what science says is the essence of well-being, or flourishing. We'll call it joy.

In the pages ahead, I've laid out the framework to allow you to know in the marrow of your bones more of who you are, what makes you so exquisitely you, and how to sow more meaning and goodness into your everyday life. That's how you find your joy spot!

Discover yourself, your goodness, and your bliss.

Let's find your joy spots! They're waiting for you!!

Chapter 1 (M/A)

You Are Pure YUM

You, beloved, are made for greatness.

Before you start looking behind you, wondering who I might be talking about, I'm talking to you.

You.

You were made with specific gifts and talents that were meant to make the world a better place.

How can you serve the world by playing small?

Maybe you even notice the whisper or perhaps the shout of that voice inside of you saying,

"Try this…"

"Try that…"

"Wouldn't it be great if…"

"I'd love to…"

If you stopped what you were doing and listened to that voice, how would you end those sentences?

What would you do if you knew you would succeed and couldn't fail?

What can you do, with intention, daily, to honour that nudge?

If you're having trouble hearing that voice, listen to what others say about you when you shine. Maybe it's something like this:

"You're so creative!"

"You're such a great writer!"

"You're such a talented designer!"

"You sure know how to get things off the ground!"

What holds you back from letting their words sink in?

You, and only you, bring something very special into this world.

A *light* that only you can shine.

Your *greatness* is your purpose. It's why you're here.

L I S T E N

Don't dim your light.

Let it shine.

Follow that nudge and give in. In doing so, you're giving others permission to do the same.

You've got one chance with this precious life. Don't waste it.

It takes courage to live your life on purpose.

Chose courage today and get on your way!

This book is not pixie dust and fairy tales. The pages are mixed with personal stories, reflections, solidly research-based tools, and a scientifically validated framework of well-being. It is the real deal. The contents will transform your life.

Look, I've worked with people who have faced what seemed like insurmountable challenges. I've worked with blind people, people with chronic illnesses, clients who had months to live, leaders who were doing their best to lead their teams through a pandemic (did you ever think we would be navigating a pandemic?).

I've worked with business owners who are incredibly successful and want to do even more for themselves and the community they serve. I've worked with staff from huge hotel and restaurant chains and worked with surgeons and staff from some of the biggest hospitals in the world.

I've worked with MANY people who are all so different, and ALL so the same. They want a delicious life, and they want to make a difference. They want their life to feel valuable and they want to feel good while they are doing all the things they do.

That's why I know what I do because those lovelies are all vastly different and so very much the same.

So, there you have it.

As you go through each chapter you can journal your answers, think about them without writing, or discuss your answers with a friend or partner. (I mentioned that in the introduction, but if you're like me, I've never read an introduction in my life, so I'm repeating it here.)

If you go through it and you don't feel extra deliciousness seep into your life-send it back-full refund!

Reflections

Complete the sentence stems.

I'd love to try...

Wouldn't it be great if...?

I'd love to...

I stand for...

I want more...

I am curious about...

Now take a couple of these answers and get moving.

What will you do to make these things happen?

Chapter 2 (P)

Joy-Is That You?

I've been giving a lot of thought as to why I am so freakin' fascinated by joy.

When I hear people talk about finding joy, or feeling joy, I feel like jumping up and down and yelling "YES!" In fact, I have done just that!

I've worked with clients where they've had the courage to not only start a business, but after a year of working together, without working more hours, they've doubled their income. Now they have more freedom and are feeling overjoyed!

Or my favourite, they had been working 80 hours a week and now they're working 40 hours a week without a drop in revenue. YES PLEASE!

I have run through my house clapping as I see people reach the goodness that they long for.

I am committed to helping people create more joy in their lives and bring more joy into their lives, businesses, teams, and families. Why? Because I know full well that joy is the magic juice that makes all the difference.

Happiness and joy lead to better health, lower stress, increased productivity, decreased pain, increased resilience, and heck, it even dilates blood vessels, and that's just the tip of the iceberg! I'll have some of that. Yes please!

What makes me so intensely joy full is that I vividly remember a time when I didn't know joy. During those days, I would lie in my closet and cry, wishing I could fall asleep and never wake up. My marriage was falling apart, I had been deeply betrayed and my world had been turned upside down.

My heart was shattered and I did not know how I would make it some days.

The only thing that kept me going for many months was my kids.

I knew I would survive but…

I came out of the closet. (Not in the commonly used sense, although I considered many options while I was serving my time and that did cross my mind. ;)

I crawled out.

NEVER expecting to find joy.

NEEEEEEEVVVVVVVVVVVEEEEEEEEEEEEERRRRRR-RRRRRRRRRRRR!

Guess what?

What I found on the other side of despair was deep, gurgling joy. Like the pain had carved out more space for joy.

Even better, my life was good before my time in the closet but, much to my absolute delight, I am happier now than I have ever been, or ever can even remember.

I'm so excited to wake up most mornings, I can't even sleep in because I am so thrilled about what each day holds. Who would have ever thought?!

Not me. Not ever. To go from dreaming of my death to being delighted with life feels like nothing short of a miracle. :)

Joy, to me, feels like winning the lottery.

It really is the greatest gift.

I never knew life could be so good. It's not perfect, but it is rich and so full.

I run three companies, have amazing clients, am healthy, have great kids, I work hard but never long, I walk everyday, have meaningful relationships and even a great partner. ;) That's joy.

If you're in a *closet* in an area of your life and life feels flat and dull, come out and join me. Don't spend one more minute in there. Crawl out if you need to, but do it, do it today. I've got you and you'll be delighted by what goodness is waiting for you.

Reflections

Who would you be if you experienced more joy?

How would your life be different if you had more joy?

What would you do differently if you knew joy?

What will you do today to feel some joy? (Keep it simple.)

Chapter 3 (P)

Fear, Vulnerability and Courage Walk Into a Bar

Before we dive into this chapter, let's get to know some *characters* in our stories.

Courage, Fear, and Vulnerability walk into a bar.

They sit down and order drinks. Fear orders two doubles.

They start to discuss an upcoming event and they talk about what's going on for each of them.

Vulnerability says, "I don't like the looks of this, we're going to be exposed, people will really *see* us; feels risky."

Fear says with such eloquence, "Are you KIDDING me?! There's no freakin' way I'm doing this!"

Courage says, "We're doing this."

Fear and vulnerability are cousins. They've grown up together, they've grown closer over the years, and they whisper back and forth A LOT, especially in stressful circumstances.

Fear is the less complex of the two. He sniffs out what he perceives to be dangerous from miles away and tries to get the group to turn back.

Fear's not dynamic, he doesn't explore. He says, and sometimes screams, "RUUUN!"

Vulnerability has some of Fear's DNA, they're related after all. Vulnerability knows Fear but checks things out anyway. He sees that if one is to forge ahead, try something out, or create something, there is risk.

Courage is aware of all that Vulnerability and Fear have noticed but understands that if we don't do this, we risk staying small, not truly connecting, or creating anything new or being innovative.

The cousins gulp loudly in response.

Courage allows immigrants to settle in new places, allows artists to paint, sing and dance, people to fall in love and run races. (Feel nervous just thinking about those things? That's Vulnerability and Fear doing a number on you.) For those artists, runners, and lovers it was not for lack of the warning shouts informing them of their possible demise, it was the courage to move ahead despite them.

It's taking the risk of really and truly being seen, trying something out, reaching out-whatever it might be.

It's risking flat out butt-baring nakedness, and someone seeing the truth unhidden. And that's scary, even terrifying at times.

Courage knows fear and vulnerability, and he says to them, "I know you, but let's do this anyways."

GULP. (Fear orders another double.)

Courage doesn't wipe out fear.

True courage allows us to be vulnerable despite Fear's Armageddon messages. Courage recognizes vulnerability and embraces it to say, "This feels awful but I'm going to do this, not without you, but with both of you."

When we tell someone how courageous they are, the comeback 99.9 per cent of the time is, "I don't feel courageous. I feel terrified (or afraid, or sad, or overwhelmed…)."

Brené Brown, a vulnerability researcher, says, "You can choose courage, or you can choose comfort, but you can't have both."

The truth is vulnerability is the birthplace of intimacy, true connection, creativity, and innovation.

Vulnerability allows us to create something: launch a new business, perform a song in front of a live audience, publish a blog or tell someone you love them. Vulnerability lets you put a boundary in place, deal with your declining health or hold someone's hand when they're suffering. Vulnerability means flat out, unbridled courage.

Courage is facing the cards that we've been dealt: a parent dying, a child with cancer, a car accident, or recovering from an assault.

Courage might be as simple, or as hard, as putting one foot in front of the other when the load seems too much to bear.

Courage is going on a first date after your marriage ended.

Courage is reaching out for help and letting others know that you're terrified by a recent health diagnosis.

Courage is applying for a new job after being recently laid off.

Courage is telling your friend that you're scared.

That's where courage and vulnerability come together.

Courage is not about bucking up and moving ahead without help, or strong emotions, real courage isn't as simple as that.

Courage is complex and beautiful. Courage is admirable and breathtaking.

Courage is you.

You have it in you to allow yourself to be seen; to really explore, and then really show up in all areas of your life and to truly live brave. It takes courage to allow joy into your life.

Reflections

What are you afraid of, right now?

What would you do if you weren't afraid?

What would you ask for?

What boundaries would you put in place in order to live more fully? Think of what's OK and what's not. Make decisions based on what's OK and move away from what's not OK.

Which part of your story would you embrace?

What would you love to create and put into the world?

Embrace courage and intentionally move towards creating the delicious life you've always longed for.

Chapter 4 (E)

S p a c e

As you move towards joy, you're going to need some space.

If I could put something on my Christmas list that would ensure I would feel more goodness, creative, and fulfilled every day, it would be SPACE. Space from other people. Space from work. Physical space. All kinds of space.

That's it.

Sounds simple and yet we rarely have enough of it.

We live in a busy, bustling world. We seldom get time to ourselves and when we do, it's hard to slow down so we dive into things that force us to unwind. Think of a good Netflix binge. There's nothing wrong with that, if it's done with intention, but it doesn't feel great when you realize an afternoon has been flushed away when you'd planned to only watch a few episodes.

What's the value of space?

It allows us to recharge, think and create more of what fulfills us.

It also allows us to find more joy. Now we're talking!

Space also helps us access new ideas.

You're trying to solve a problem or come up with an idea, a way of addressing an issue, and it has you stumped. Later, when you're taking a shower, or doing something else, the solution comes to you-downloaded directly into your sweet brain.

That's the power of space.

If we want to live a peace-filled, innovative, and creative life, or even tap into a part of fulfillment, we need space to make it happen.

So often, we save vacations for some space or a change of pace, but even then, we go from place, to place to explore, and we rarely have nothing to do.

Space is what we need to be more creative and innovative in order to live the thriving, purpose-filled lives that we long for.

I used to fear space. Big Time.

What if I got bored? What if space allowed for some deep dissatisfaction to surface? Those thoughts used to terrify me.

Creating space for some discomfort is far better than living a numbed-out life trying to avoid what we really need to address.

If your occupation provides deep fulfillment and you're currently licking the icing off the cake of your life while you're inhaling that cherry on top-that's great. Purpose and meaning begets purpose and meaning, so your creative sparks may always be firing. However, you'll need space to reset.

Space provides opportunity and joy.

Think of a loved one who you could just eat with a spoon-they're so yummy. Even the most delicious partner or friend connection can fade if you interact constantly.

Creating more space doesn't mean that you sit around and do nothing, although sometimes it might look like that. It means that you are intentional about creating some time to breathe and fill it with something other than day to day busyness.

Space brings with it a rich and luxurious feeling. Time is a gift and to have the space to enjoy it makes my heart sing.

The space we create can be filled with things that recharge us and are intentional. You could fill your space with:

a walk

meditation

journaling

being creative

driving without the radio on

sitting and savouring a cup of coffee

colouring

a nap

playing

Space allows for connecting with what brings you joy.

Space is meant to be a refreshing part of our lives, a place to intention-ally refuel and restore.

If space is a new concept, explore different ways to create space. For me, it starts with having 30 minutes each morning to journal, meditate, and reflect. It feels like chocolate for my soul.

Explore some ways to create your space and fill it with something that slows you down and fills you up with goodness.

If it feels uncomfortable, or even impossible, at first, start off small and do more of what makes you feel peaceful. A wee step in this direction could cause a spark of joy. A joy spot may show up.

Change up how you structure your days. Plan certain tasks on some days to free up space on another. This may be a bit of a different kind of space, but there is nothing like a day free from errands, or clients to get things done or to just be-simply delectable!

Now is a glorious time to create more space. Make room for it and savour it.

You'll become refreshed and, who knows, maybe with some new ideas to create an even more wildly fulfilling life.

What space do you need to feel more alive?

Extra time and extra space in our lives is one of the most delicious ways to measure wealth and we get it by courageously making it a priority.

Once you've created more space, create more space for joy. Get that feeling of a puppy jumping on your lap, or clearing out the clutter in your life. That's joy.

Reflections

What would more space give you?

What's one thing you would say "no" to right now to create more space?

Who do you need to let know that you need more space?

What will you do to ensure you keep your space?

What does your heart long for in that space?

Commit to the space that you create. Put it in your calendar and experi-ment with how to fill your space. You'll start to glimpse joy as you create more intentional space. It's going to be so yum.

Chapter 5 (P)

"Does This Bring Me Joy?"

I LOVE to purge and do it on a regular basis (often when I'm procrastinating). I purge closets, drawers, and business systems. Anything that can be resorted, I will do it. I did it many times while I was avoiding writing this book.

I started a new system of purging after reading a book review about a book by Marie Kondo. While going through items, she touches them and asks, "Does this spark joy?"

If it doesn't, it gets donated or tossed.

Yum!!! I didn't need to read any more to get started sparking more joy. I am in!

I went through my closet and as I looked at each piece…

Joy, joy, no joy, no joy, no joy, joy. Forty per cent of my clothes were donated that week.

GAME CHANGER!

I kept going and went through my kitchen, and then my books. I took all of my books off the shelves and gave away five bags full of books. I kept one bag. Yikes! Next, I hit my basement, my garage, and my businesses. I went through everything, getting rid of what I could to open some spaces in my life for what really matters.

This joy full way of purging was delightfully clear and a ruthless approach to an awesome decluttering project.

At one point, I was excitedly telling my kiddos what I was up to and

I jokingly grabbed my beloved daughter's ankle as she was laying on the couch. I said, "I'm only keeping the things that bring me joy and I'm on the border with some of you."

I have decided to keep her-she's a good one and brings me a lot of joy. She may still be a bit traumatized, bless her, by my joke and may be in therapy for some time.

What if you took an inventory of your things, your activities, and your life, and focused on what really brought you joy?

Kept what lit you up and purged some of the things that didn't?

Do you hear courage whispering your name?

This isn't about fairies and pixie dust; it's about creating a life that's genuinely filled with purpose and meaning.

That's the birthplace of joy.

So, get to it. Start in one wee way today, maybe clear off your desk, and then keep moving! Take before and after pictures. That's how you capture your joy spots and savour them.

Reflections

Ask yourself one simple question:

Does this bring me joy?

Where will you start?

List all the items, relationships, and tasks that you want to purge. Suggestions:

- Get rid of the stuff-don't complicate things. Minimalist experts say if it's worth less than $50, donate it as it's not worth your time to post it and deal with the buyers.

- If you haven't used an item in 90 days, and you can get it again in less than 20 minutes for less than $20, get rid of it. You're looking differently at your turkey baster, aren't you?

I've done this and it's funny how I have never missed my turkey baster or the two million screws and nails I housed in my garage. Do it with friends and share some before and after pics. Heck-send me some pics. Shared joy is joy squared.

Finding some joy spots already? Of course, you are!!

Chapter 6 (E)

Who Were You When This First Started?

This is the grit that made you who you are today.

I can hear it play in the background. I have a song in my head. "Let's start at the very beginning" from the *Sound of Music*.

SORRY! I know you can hear Maria singing in your ear, too.

Now the song is probably stuck in your head.

Dang *Sound of Music* soundtrack!

In order to move forward, we need to look back.

Think back to when you were a kid, maybe four or five-years-old. This was usually a time when you felt alive and full of life and energy.

Even better, find a pic of your wee self. You were a delightful, playful lamb at this point.

You were full of life and all the things that made the world a better place to be. My picture would show sunshine, play, a banana seat bike (just dated myself,) and pure goodness.

That wee kiddo is still inside you. These wee selves hold a lot of wisdom even for us now.

We changed as we got older, sometimes for the better, sometimes because of being hurt and guarding our hearts. The light of our inner child may have dimmed, but it is longing to return.

Find a picture of yourself as a kid and think back to what gave you joy. What did you do to foster more joy and fun when you were a wee lamb?

What part of that younger self would you like to give more space to in your life now?

Reflections

Who were you when you felt most alive when you were little?

What were you like?

What did you love doing?

What did you do in your free time?

What would play look like for you at this age?

What do you need now to play more?

What's one thing you're willing to add to your life to honour that inner, wise, playful kiddo?

Chapter 7 (M)

Our Stories

The stories that shaped us as kids and formed the foundation of who we became.

My home was a stable, loving, and traditional home. My dad worked outside the home while my mom worked in the home. She was the glue of our family. She was pure joy. She was filled with gratitude and seemingly endless happiness.

I remember so distinctly a night that my mom was making dinner and it seemed to be taking forever. The whole family was seated in the kitchen, at the table, and my mom KEPT getting up and leaving the kitchen and coming back to pick up where she'd left off.

I remember feeling something was off, but I was eight, and I couldn't figure it out. I woke up the next day and my dad told me that mom was in the hospital. She was to have surgery to remove a brain tumour.

She'd been sick the day before, and sick for a while apparently, and we, as her kids, had no clue. She was delayed in prepping dinner the previous night because she had an incredibly bad headache and was going to the bathroom to throw up. (OK-WHO DOES THAT?)

Life changed immediately then. Without my mom to support my dad, things started to disintegrate.

I knew the surgery would be serious, but not as serious as when one night, shortly after my mom went into the hospital, I woke up to dad pulling back the covers and crying with his head on my chest. My dad was weeping about how his wife was going to die. I consoled him quietly but, in my heart, I was screaming at him.

"Who cares about your wife! THAT'S MY MOM! That's my mommy who's going to die."

If I had known a swear word at that time, I would have used it. I wanted to shove him away, tell him to eff off and scream that his wife was my mom, and my mom COULDN'T die. I NEEDED HER.

Yet I set aside my own feelings and gently comforted him.

My mother's seemingly imminent death was reinforced days later when we were taken to the hospital.

"Tell Mom that you love her and say goodbye as she probably won't survive the surgery," were our dire instructions.

It was the worst. I was hysterical when I said goodbye to her. I had to be pried off her. Mom was calm, peaceful, and her normal self.

I knew what it would be like to be left with my dad. When my mom was in the hospital, my dad wasn't my dad. He wasn't the same man as when my mom was around. He was overwhelmed and leaned on me for support.

I was eight.

My mom ended up doing OK and came home to us. Thankfully.

I know you've got a story as well. I am sorry for what broke you and your heart when you were young. I know. Our stories form and shape us and become part of our make up.

Knowing that others have more painful stories makes me want to shrink back from my own.

"It's hardly anything, Leona," I tell myself. "It's fine."

I've said that to myself my whole life.

Far worse things have happened to many other people. OH, I know this. I know this very well. Hearing horrible, tragic, and upsetting stories has made me feel like a loser for letting my story bother me.

Knowing another's pain and comparing it to my own has alienated me from my story. When I do that, I'm not giving my story the space it needs to show me how it has impacted me.

I have made conscious choices to work with what has happened to me.

Comparative suffering, according to Brené Brown, is where we minimize our own experiences because there is always someone with a worse story. It keeps us from owning our own story, honouring that experience along with the tough emotions that come with it, and integrating that truth into our lives.

I give myself permission to own my story and the fact that it changed my make up.

I saw it even this morning as I write this chapter. I feel how deeply it has impacted my life. It doesn't have to be the *worst* experience to alter things.

This story of how I needed to support my dad when he was upset has played out in my first marriage. It felt like my job to support my husband without good boundaries or expressing my own needs. I ended up in a 19-year marriage where my "job" was to support my husband, too. It was not a true partnership, but I didn't know that wasn't even normal.

My model was girls/women supported men. They lean, we support-NEVER, or very rarely, is it the other way around. My mom supported my dad and when she wasn't around, it was my responsibility.

That story ran my life. It has cost me a lot. It has also taught me a great deal now that I am aware of it.

You have a story that shaped you. In fact, most likely more than one story. Those hard things can become a gift when given the chance.

Reflections

You don't need to think of something extremely painful, but perhaps an experience from your childhood came up as you read this chapter.

How did this experience shape you?

How does it still impact you?

What messages did you take on as a result of what happened to you as a child?

What situations cause these childhood feelings to rise up for you?

Is there something you would tell that kiddo to comfort them?

You never need to get over something that has happened to you. You may always feel triggered, angry, or loss over something that happened. Our role is to honour that pain and integrate that story into our lives so we can respond to it, ask those who love us to support us, and to respond to that pain. This work is for the brave. Go gently.

Chapter 8 (M)

You Do What?

While my mother was in the hospital, my dad gave me the job of calling relatives with updates. I was put in my parents' room with a list of family members' phone numbers.

I was eight. This was bananas, but I did it because that's what good girls do. What they're told.

I relayed the information over and over again.

"My mom is sick. She could die."

My relatives would ask to talk to my dad, and I'd say he couldn't come to the phone as he was worried he would cry and wouldn't be able to get the words out to talk to them.

This story of my eight-year-old self has played out over and over in my life. When something happens, especially involving sickness or death, I go into overdrive. I call everyone, arrange things, and manage the situation.

Years later, my brother was sick (ironically with a brain tumour), and I went into hyper-drive. My husband at the time said, "What are you doing? You don't have to manage all of this. Do you see what you're doing?"

I stopped dead.

I was the eight-year-old, acting EXACTLY as I did then.

Taking it all on, managing it, doing a lot, feeling little and being driven by my past and my reaction to the feelings it brought up.

Harriet Lerner says in her book, *The Dance of Connection*, that in anxious situations we show up in one of two ways; as an overfunctioner or an underfunctioner.

Overfunctioners do a lot in stressful situations and don't allow themselves to feel.

Underfunctioners do little and feel overwhelmed by their feelings.

If you are the oldest female in your family, you're most likely an overfunctioner. Eighty per cent of first-born females are overfunctioners. AHEM… that's me.

My name is Leona and I OVERFUNCTION. If I am stressed, I don't slow down, I speed up without thinking. It's unconscious. Some people disappear in high stress. They underfunction. We all have our roles.

A while back, I was struggling with chronic pain. I couldn't even lift a jug of milk, and I was a couple of days away from throwing a fundraiser for over 100 people. That's when I got a call from my son.

"I think the sewer backed up," he said.

I got home and sure enough, there was crap all over the floor. Literally.

I got into the "mode." I assessed the situation, looked at all I had on my plate that week, how I felt physically, and I got into fix-it-mode.

I didn't panic at all. In fact, I felt very little. I got tunnel vision and I accessed what needed to happen to manage the crisis. Overfunctioners access situations quickly and take control so they can try to avert what seems like an imminent crisis. I do this very well.

As I was driving to my partner's house, I felt like I had an impenetrable dome over my head; I felt little, I felt numb and I thought to myself, "I feel like I'm eight. Exactly like when my mom was sick."

I had never thought that before. I think I may have felt more like my eight-year-old self because of the vulnerability of my being physically impaired. I don't think I would have noticed otherwise.

I was in crisis management mode. In this state, I get extremely calm, put things in order and carry on. I don't talk much, and I don't let anyone in.

There was no room for anyone else in this model. My partner was talking about how he would help; what he could do, but I wouldn't let him help.

I told myself, "I can do this. I will do this despite my pain."

My partner wanted to share the load with me. Nevertheless, I felt like I couldn't let him in because my story is *men lean in when you're already overwhelmed.*

So, I blocked him out.

I knew he was beside me, but I couldn't take in his words. He sounded like Charlie Brown's teacher.

Later, he told me that it was like I had some impenetrable shield around me.

I battened down the hatches. Got extremely calm. Got extremely logical.

Then, I was blindsided with the truth.

"You don't let anyone in," he said.

It was so obvious he was right.

I started crying. (I'm choked up now remembering his words.) In my overfunctioning mode, I can't lean on anyone. Not the good, the safe or the extremely capable, and I certainly don't know how to feel or be loved in times of high stress.

It began with my story, my old story. It was holding me back from sharing the burden. It was mitigating something that makes me feel terrifyingly vulnerable, but it was also keeping me from experiencing life altering love. Love that could strengthen my bones and make my heart more whole.

I felt alone and no one could get past that impenetrable shield. I HAD no idea I was building barriers. In my past relationships with men, I never had someone who wanted to shoulder some of my responsibilities. I didn't even know what that felt like or even how to be open to that. It was literally unknown to me.

Now I'm getting help to lean into love in all times. I am laying down my overfunctioning shield and letting feelings in. Not just the anxious feelings but the feelings of love and support, the safe place to fall that I so desperately need.

Overfunctioning is not all bad, it's the awareness that brings us back to our equilibrium. My healing is in recognizing the unconscious drives in my life and what brought me here, so I can respond to myself with compassion and change my ways. I still know how to get things done, but I also know the feeling of when I am reacting, taking over situations, and not allowing myself the space to feel.

For us in the overfunctioning camp, we need to slow down, do less and feel more. I struggle with that. I am learning to do less but when you haven't allowed yourself to feel a lot of sadness for most of your life, it's hard to be OK with that.

I'm learning.

Underfunctioners tend to feel more overwhelmed and they tend to avoid addressing the stressful situation. You might notice that they are less engaged, withdraw, are late for things, shirk responsibilities, and pull way back.

The antidote for an underfunctioner is to do a bit more and not give into the feelings so much. Your team, family, and community need you. I can let go of the overfunctioning and underfunction when it comes to dealing with conflict. I don't want to enter a conversation that feels really vulnerable and deal with the feelings that an unsettled situation brings up for me, so I withdraw from the relationship, or situation. I am learning not to do that any longer as well.

We can each overfunction or underfunction based on the circumstances. Whether you're an over or underfunctioner, know you're normal, we all do it, AND by being more aware of when we do it, we can respond to stressful situations more effectively. There's a joy spot there!

Reflections

Think about how you respond to stressful situations.

Are you an overfunctioner or an underfunctioner?

How do those traits show up and what are they keeping you from?

What do you need to come back to more balance and a place that allows you to do a bit of something and, at the same time, feel what you need to feel in a healthy way?

Most of all, be gentle with yourself. This is a hero's journey, your story of grit to grace.

Chapter 9 (M)

What You Model They Become

I used to think my mom was a saint. Well, she's dead now and if that qualifies her for sainthood, she is one. (Although I'm no saint expert.)

My siblings and I put her on a pedestal. If you had met my mother, you might put her there, too. She was "that" mom. She was very loving, happy, and infinitely grateful.

When she was 24, it was discovered that she had a life-threatening brain tumour on her brainstem. My momma, who had two wee boys at the time, was given a 10 per cent chance of survival. She told her best friend that she just wanted to see her kids grow up and that she was scared of leaving them motherless.

I didn't know that scared part of my mom. Not one ounce of it.

I knew the mom who made us dinner while she was gravely ill, to her own demise.

My mom didn't fake joy or happiness, she wasn't inauthentic in that. She had brushed death's door early in her life and she was so grateful everyday.

The GIFT of life was not lost on her. EVER.

To grow up in the presence of such gratitude was a blessing.

She died when I was 22. She was 49. The age I am as I write this chapter.

My mom, our mom, could do no wrong. She loved us, listened to us, and was so kind and nurturing and that stays with me today. She loved everyone. Our home was open to all and we, more often than not, had a dinner table filled with friends.

She left another mark, too. A shadowy side to all this goodness that we also bear to this day.

It took a long time to notice it.

We NEVER saw her sweat. EVER. (OK maybe once.) She seemed to not let anything bother her.

We only saw her get choked up once. ONCE.

After a brain surgery, because she couldn't sleep and hadn't slept in a couple of nights, she got choked up. Some doctor told her to have a strong drink and see if that helped. She never drank and here she was choking back a vodka and orange juice. She was teary-eyed because she hated feeling this way.

It was terrifying to see her "crack" even a bit in that moment. Our mom did not show us this part of herself, ever.

She wouldn't take sleeping pills or pain meds when she didn't feel good because she would soldier through anything. She was "strong" and didn't want help. So here she was with a drink in her hand and showing us her vulnerable side. It felt like the sky was falling to see her like that.

My mom did not have an easy life. My dad was a workaholic and she had 10 brain surgeries in 25 years. We often didn't have much money and had a family of four kids.

My mom was always on the move, even while she was sick. She laid down when she was in the hospital. That's it. She even made lunch for us right after she had an aneurysm. She'd felt a pop in her head and felt searing pain. She knew that something was gravely wrong and that she needed to get to the hospital, but delayed the trip to feed us (WHAT THE HECK?), and then had eight hours of brain surgery after lunch. I was 16 and very capable of fending for myself. She may have been the captain of the overfunctioning team and we loved her for it.

She let us cry. She let us be sick and she was so tender in her care, BUT she never even laid down, she never slowed down, she never cried, except the one time.

What she modelled; we became.

We did not take on the behaviours of what she gave us permission for, we took on her behaviours: *don't feel sad, always be grateful and do not rest. EVER.* (Can you see the overfunctioning recipe unfolding?)

She NEVER asked for help. EVER. If she could have driven herself to the hospital in that moment of her brain bleed, she would have.

She did not show that she was vulnerable.

That was her shadow.

We took on that to be strong, you don't rest, you don't get help, you don't lean in. You don't feel darker emotions. No sadness, no talk of struggle, no processing of hard things.

This lack of vulnerability showed up in our lives and is still a struggle. We don't do sadness. We don't know how to give heartache space. However, I'm learning. My dad's sadness was so terrifying that it reinforced my mom's apparent wisdom in not letting any sort of sorrow show.

We tough it out, often with a smile on our faces.

When I was 22, we were told she was dying. She had a breathing tube in her throat so she could not talk; we said goodbye and she was all smiles. Who reacts like this? We checked and she was not on meds that would make her feel loopy. She had refused any meds, in fact. She was grateful for her life, not one indication of the pain of leaving us was reflected in her attitude, like she couldn't feel that part. She rallied and died a few weeks later.

As her children became adults, the shadow of our upbringing has remained with us.

Be busy.

Don't slow down.

Don't take help.

Don't stop, don't feel, keep going.

I still struggle with feeling lazy when I rest. I feel inadequate when I get tired and don't feel like doing anything. Don't get me started about sitting down and watching TV.

When I sit, I feel like my worth decreases exponentially. I got that from my mom. This doesn't change how I feel about her. She was goodness wrapped up in a momma, but she had her flaws, and this was one of them. I am learning to undo some of that legacy that she left us with.

I used to not take medication when I was sick, I just toughed it out. Natural childbirth? Of course. People who lie down or take a day off for a cold? PFFT-that's for the weak.

"We" lie down when we have brain surgery. Not before. You can work through a flu, a cold, or whatever life throws your way.

Listen to what your body wants more of? That's for the wimps. My mom would NEVER have done that.

She toughed it out and some of this may have even led to her demise. Might she have lived longer if she had rested more, gotten more help, didn't soldier through, and made herself a priority? Maybe. I don't judge her. She did what she knew.

What changed for me was I didn't want to live like that-to live in a grind, to not give myself permission to rest, or feel my feelings, or ask for help. I was and am done.

If we want our people, our kids, those we lead on our teams, to be a certain way, we need to not only speak the words of what we want, but we need to model the behaviours that we want to see in others.

If we want our people to live a balanced life, we must model that.

If we want our loves to speak kindly about themselves, we must model that self compassion. If we want them to be or do something in a specific way, we must, very carefully, model that which will make them healthy individuals.

What we model, they become. What we give ourselves permission for, they too give themselves permission to do. There is hope in that.

Reflections

What was modelled to you as a child?

What parts of the modelling have shown up, or still do, in your behaviour or your beliefs?

What permission will you give yourself to change that?

Is there something you want to do differently to enable you to move towards what you need and away from how you were raised?

How will this help you?

Chapter 10 (M)

Dear 15-Year-Old Self

What would you say to your 15-year-old self?

(You can pick any age where the child-like light starts to dim and you feel that childish joy fade.)

I bet you'd have a lot to say to your teenage self.

When I was asked that question, I unexpectedly felt such sadness well up in me. It was unusual, as it was a simple question. It opened a window and allowed me a glimpse of something that I didn't even know existed.

With tears streaming down my cheeks, I recalled what I was like when I was 15. I was doing everything to fit in. I wore the tight jeans, spent countless hours on my hair and makeup. I starved myself to stay a certain size. I did all I could to try to be perfect. I was so insecure and uncertain of myself.

What wouldn't leave me after I considered the question was how hollow I felt at that age. When only a decade before I was soooo full. I was a joy filled, courageous five-year-old kiddo. It seemed like at 15, that was all gone.

I made myself look good every day-for the approval of boys, who later became the men in my life. I had very little idea that I was here for more than that.

My mom had given up her education to take care of her much younger siblings and she gave up a lot to take care of our family as I was growing up.

I took on the notion from her and my grandmothers, that women sacrifice; we give up things for the betterment of others. We matter less than others.

That breaks my heart.

At 15, I believed that in order to be enough I had to empty myself of me, to fit in, to be "loved."

So, I emptied myself of my own value.

I bet some of you did, too.

I didn't know then what I had emptied out. I came from a culture that valued hard work and, no matter what, keep moving-don't stop.

I emptied and married without finishing my education. I had babies and I emptied more, always striving to be what I thought was a great mom and a perfect wife-working hard and serving the needs of everyone before me.

I didn't even notice me.

I became a scrap of myself in my 20s. I poured myself out so the mould I was so desperately trying to fill would be perfect, would be enough, and I would find the love and the security that I so desperately sought.

When I was 30 with three kids, I was diagnosed with the same genetic condition that my mother had died of. I was terrified. I knew the life expectancy, which was 49.

Yet I didn't stop to fill myself up or to nurture my soul. Instead, I cleaned my house and prepared food so if my first scans showed some awful tumours, I would be no trouble for those people who might need to help me out.

It sounds ridiculous but I cleaned every cabinet so no one would see that they were messy or disorganized. At one point, I had made 23 frozen casseroles so if I got sick, no one would have to cook for me or my family for a while.

Within months of that diagnosis, I suffered from unexplained chronic pain, severe anxiety, and got influenza that I could not recover from. Eventually, I developed a heart condition and lost 30 pounds.

I wore makeup and nice clothes everyday. Even during my illness, regardless of how I felt, to prove I was enough.

I never slept in or got rid of anything on my overflowing plate. I took one day off in that six-month period and I always kept trying to look good and keep moving-my life's mantra.

I never once realized how empty I was. I was too busy. I had to be enough. That was all. I worked hard, tried to look good and, surely, that made me worthy of love and belonging. I learned this young and it has taken me years to shed this belief.

Reflections

What would you say to your teenage self?

What beliefs did you take on as a kid?

How did that shape who you became?

Would you be willing to change any behaviours that you took on when you were younger, and don't serve you anymore?

Don't worry, we ARE getting to the joy part. We need to make some space for it and clean up some cobwebs first. This is the gritty part.

Chapter 11 (P)

Not Even Close

When I had been married for 16 years, I found out that my husband was having an affair.

It confirmed my worst fear.

I WAS NOT ENOUGH!!!!

Not even one bit enough.

I knew I wasn't smart enough, thin enough, or young enough. The "not enough" list was endless.

Who would want me?

I could work, stay thin, be a decent mom, and yet I was so deeply flawed. That's how I felt.

My 15-year-old self, who focused so much on trying to be perfect and always felt like she had failed, was right. The same truth I knew then was now bubbling up in this scenario.

Be pretty, play small, you don't matter all that much.

I took on lies; I took on the notion that being a living shell of a being is OK as long as you appeared a certain way and served others well.

It was all a big, fat, empty lie and I gobbled it up.

I look back at that 15-year-old kiddo and I shout at her until my voice grows hoarse and her ears ring:

"YOU MATTER!"

"YOU'RE ENOUGH!"

I'd tell her that she's free to be who she was made to be-don't play small.

"Your flaws don't define you!"

"You're meant to be full, happy, fulfilled!"

If I could, I'd take that girl onto my lap and I'd love her back to life, kiss both of her eyelids so she could see her worth and the beauty that has nothing to do with the way she looks, and I would whisper into her ear, "You belong, you matter, you are deeply loved."

Had that 15-year-old known her worth, her life would have turned out very differently.

I don't just say that to her, I say that to you.

You are worthy of the deepest love.

You are perfectly imperfect and so much more beautiful and exquisite because of it.

You are to be cherished and held in the highest esteem.

You are remarkably you.

So, I ask you, what does your 15-year-old self need to hear?

Don't leave those words at your adolescent feet.

Listen to them, eat them up, and lather your soul with their truth. Wash away the lies that you took on to survive.

Let your words bring the dying parts of you back to life.

Bring to the world all of you, every last saucy bit.

Reflections

What happened that made you think you weren't enough?

Where did your "not enoughness" show up then?

Where does it show up now?

When you don't listen to where you feel like you're not enough, what's the beautiful truth about you?

Finish these sentence stems about the truth of who you are:

I am…

I am…

I am…

Keep going! You don't have to be perfect to be worthy of all that your heart aches for.

Chapter 12 (P)

Go Deeper

Let's go deeper. We've all been betrayed, overlooked, wounded beyond measure.

What was it for you?

For me I knew it. As I've mentioned, I thought I wasn't smart enough, thin enough, young enough, energetic enough, independent enough, and spunky enough. The list was endless.

I'd felt it for my whole life, but I felt like anyone could smell the ripeness of this putrid truth on my skin then, and for many years to follow.

I wasn't enough of so many things that would make it possible for someone to love me unconditionally. Who would want me?

The affair was my worst fear confirmed. After 16 years of what I thought was a good marriage, his affection turned toward another, AND it was because I wasn't enough.

That's how I felt anyways.

Everything that I had hoped would never see the light of day was now blinding me. My husband cared for another. I wanted to die. And for a long time, I was welcoming that opportunity.

After my ex-husband's affair, I thought of writing a book and calling the first chapter "Cellulite and Wrinkles." I thought it was fitting as that was all I could see when I looked in the mirror. All I thought of were my flaws, all that made me clearly unlovable. I would use the chapter to write about my "uglies" and I would feel redeemed by spotlighting my shame.

I did a lot of work to climb out of my pile-driven-shame-hole, a hole that I had dug most of myself.

We all have those nasty places that we try to keep hidden. We feel like imposters when we get a certain job. We feel vulnerable when we wear a bathing suit (or terrified). We fear that we ARE too sensitive, and no one will love us just the way we are.

We don't work hard enough, or we work too hard.

We are too fat, or too bony, or too loud, or too awkward.

We are not enough and too much of something all at the same time. If someone finds out (and it's worse if that someone is someone we love, or someone that our livelihood depends on), we're laid bare and fear we will be turfed out on the street, smeared with shame.

We fear that our inadequacies will be brought to the light and we will burn in their truth.

BUT... what if that's all a lie?

What if it is our vulnerabilities that make us beautiful and unique and true?

What if it is our quirks and sensitive souls that actually fill this dim world with light?

What if, while we are so desperately tying to fit in, we stumble upon the few with whom we belong? What if some extra pounds and a boisterous personality are just what makes us deliciously lovable and more than worthy of desire and true love?

What if we allow ourselves to show up and be seen for who we really are, and we shine a light into the world that only we can shine?

What if, by living out loud, with all the lights on, in the most brave and courageous way, we give others courage to do the same?

We weren't meant to be perfect; we were meant to be us.

Flaws and all.

Cellulite and wrinkles.

It's all shame.

And shame, my beloveds, is a bastard.

Shame is a liar. It whispers that we aren't enough. It yells at us from a mountain top, "YOU'RE NOT ENOUGH!!!"

Just when we're about to apply for a new job, go on a first date, or deal with a terrifying health diagnosis.

That's when we hide, shrink, shrivel, and don't risk the vulnerability of being seen.

The vaccine for shame's "taunts" is self-compassion that warmly rubs your arm and says, "Oh honey, of course you're afraid-this is terrifying but so are so many good things; show up and at least try."

The salve of empathy also comes from another courageous soul that walks alongside you and says, "Me too. I know that darkness, that slimy pit of 'not enough,' and you're not alone."

Suddenly, shame's grip is loosened, and its chokehold is not so tight.

Perfectionism, shame's sultry side kick, is suddenly not so appealing.

Just because things don't always go our way, and we are clearly not perfect-we are enough. In fact, we are beautifully and belovedly imperfect.

We are smart enough, good enough and worthy enough to live a life of courage and truth. As we own that, others will walk alongside us in the brave marriage of courage and vulnerability, to create a small revolution of brave warriors that make a new, whole-hearted world.

Let's lay down our shields, lay down our swords of perfectionism and lower our defences. Real life, rich living, true love, and joy are on the other side.

Take up courage, embrace bravery; show up and risk being seen-that's where real living begins.

Shame is indeed a sneaky bastard. It riddles our lives with *shoulds* (to start with) and grows deep roots of secrets and judgments.

One way to soften shame is with permission.

We'll go deeper into shame and mitigating its harshness but, for now, start with what those harsh voices in your head that say what YOU SHOULD do or be.

Make a list of those *shoulds*.

Mine, back then, during that affair, would have looked like:

You should have been a more attentive wife.

You should have been more interesting.

You should have noticed the signs that things weren't going well.

My permissions, if I knew of such grace, might have looked like:

Permission to love my partner and be attentive to both of our needs.

Permission to speak about what interests me.

Permission to notice what I noticed and not beat myself up for not seeing warning signs.

Today, my "shoulds" show up as:

You should be more organized.

You should work harder.

You should be more articulate.

My permissions now look like:

Permission to not be perfectly organized and let some things go.

Permission to work less than full-time hours.

Permission to respond the best I can in the moment.

Reflections

Where do you feel like you aren't enough?

What would you say, with love, to a friend who feels inadequate in the same way you do? Try talking to yourself like that.

Shoulds show up where there is shame.

What are some of the *shoulds* that are a result of something painful in your past, that perhaps holds you back now?

Write yourself a permission slip to add some ease.

Where do the *shoulds* haunt you now?

What can you give yourself permission for now?

Write it on a note and put it somewhere you can see it.

Chapter 13 (M)

What Would You Write on a Sidewalk?

A couple of years ago, I was working with a group of kids in a youth leadership program. We talked about the messages that we told ourselves that weren't kind and, ultimately, weren't the truth about us.

I had them grab a piece of chalk and write those messages on the sidewalk. These kids were in elementary school and early junior high, not very old, and yet they knew the messages loud and clear.

They wrote:

I am dumb.

I'm not pretty.

I'm not smart enough.

I'm stupid.

I was shocked that they didn't have to think twice about the things they told themselves and how courageous they were to write them out so boldly.

I was also heartbroken to see that they thought things like this at such a young age.

These kiddos were amazing, beautiful, smart, kind, courageous game-changers. They'd all participated in this leadership program and in return, they'd agreed to find a way to raise money, or collect socks, for a non-profit that I run in my free time called JoySocks. Some of the kids had raised over $1,000 and others had collected 500 pairs of socks.

These ones were going to, and already had, moved mountains.

I wish they could see what I saw in them.

These kids were ahead of the game in so many ways-they weren't afraid to air their shame: the fear of not being enough. And that's the first step to taking the wind out of the sails of those gremlins that tell us dirty little lies about ourselves.

The kids didn't talk about these messages in front of just anyone, however, they told a group of kids, whom they could trust and who were on the same page. Without that trust, we risk being overexposed, and increasing the shame.

The kids were offered empathy by each other and, by seeing that most of the messages were so similar, the shame dissipated. They realized they were not alone.

The kids and I were talking about those places where we felt like we weren't enough. We talked about being kind to ourselves and talking to ourselves like we would talk to someone we loved. This is one of the keys to self-compassion and, ultimately, self-confidence. We spoke about how we would talk to a friend if they were struggling.

We then took water balloons and threw them at the lies written on the sidewalk and spoke words of kindness to ourselves. We proclaimed the truth of who we were as we wiped out the lies with the truth and the water erased the shame.

I was so grateful that these kids were ahead of the curve, understanding the lies that could hold them back from really showing up in their lives. I was so proud of their bravery to boldly proclaim the untruths and then wipe them out in unison.

We could all fill a length of sidewalk with what makes us feel like we aren't enough. Sometimes the messages are so subtle, we don't even notice them, but they become as true as the skin we wear. They hijack us from living boldly and bravely; they can keep us hidden and sometimes afraid.

I wish that you could see all the grace and beauty and smarts that you possess and that you could be free of your "sidewalk message," too. If we don't work through all these messages, there will be little space for joy.

The next time you feel anxious, uncertain, or afraid, slow down and pull the gooey self-deprecating leeches off your brain and your soul.

Tell someone you trust about those shameful messages you carry so they can show you empathy and you can know that you're not alone. We all struggle, we all share this stuff. We all can work through this mess and live a more courageous life. We need empathy, a "me too" in that moment.

When we notice the messages about being unworthy, we need to be our own best friend. We need to talk to ourselves gently, like you would a friend, and know that the stories that we make up about being the only ones who feel like *this* (whatever *this* is) are a flat out lie.

We all share shame and the more we bring it to the light, bathe it in love, and truth, the less it has power over us.

Take your water balloon and wipe out the messages that you're not enough for whatever it is you're faced with and tell yourself the truth of who you are. If shame creeps back up, which it will (these creeps are slimy), repeat the antidote. You might just discover that, over time, you're feeling the joy, certainty, and bravery to be boldly, more beautifully you.

The world needs more of that.

Reflections

What messages would you write about yourself on a sidewalk?

I'm…….

I'm not________________enough.

I'm not________________enough.

What are some things you struggle with around not feeling or being enough?

What are your "truth water balloons" that wash away those lies?

Who are you really?

What gifts do you bring to the world?

Chapter 14 (M)

My Skirt on Sideways

What others think about us does matter. Gosh, I wish it didn't. If you're all past not caring what others think, good for you. I doubt it's actually true. If your next performance review goes poorly, what would that feel like?

Perceptions do matter to us.

For me, professionally as a leadership and business coach, I wanted to be perceived somewhere between an accountant and a lawyer. The hybrid that I've aimed for in the past appeared to be confident, knowledgeable, with a keen attention to detail.

I wanted to dot all my i's and cross all my t's before anyone knew that it was even necessary. I wanted to speak with eloquence, to show up at my clients' offices in a conservative blue suit, be poised and prepared for anything that came my way.

That was it. Not much to ask.

Except, if you've spent five minutes (OK maybe two) with me, you'd know that couldn't be further from the truth.

I don't do details and I've shocked even myself when, in the past, I've met someone in person for the first time and hugged them as soon as I saw them. It doesn't always happen, but when it does, I'm sometimes even shocked that I jumped right in for the squeeze.

Don't get me wrong, I know lawyers and accountants come in a variety of shapes, sizes, and with a wide variety of personalities, but I still don't fit the mould.

I don't do math and I don't feel very articulate at times. Conflict is so not my thing, or spreadsheets-the list is LONG PEOPLE! You get the point.

I went for an interview a couple of years into my coaching career, for a contract to coach a VP in a large organization. The CEO met me, and I was starched up and well prepared. It was so hard to stay "corseted" up. I could barely breathe, which is exactly what I wanted.

I walked in, imprisoned in a façade. I had stuffed myself meticulously into all the weak spots in my costume where *Leona, the smart, yet often funny one*, might escape.

As the universe would have it, I left the office with my skirt on sideways. The joke was on me. I'd twisted myself into something I was not, and my skirt couldn't even keep from contorting itself.

I vowed to never do that again. I felt like a fraud for not being authentic and I hated being all "tied" up to get a contract.

What was I hiding? What was I so committed to keeping behind closed doors?

Me.

The *Me* that was so far from being what I was so committed to appear like. I made sure I wasn't funny or too warm. I made sure I wasn't myself.

I couldn't do it again. It was fake and so far from my integrity. The truth is, I love people. I do know to shake hands with people upon meeting them, but to be honest, many meetings do end with a hug-that's me.

I love connecting genuinely. I have strong leadership and business expertise; I can have an intelligent conversation and I have great business acumen. I also get choked up easily, I laugh heartily, have a good sense of humour, and have fun, all while getting some serious work done. I tend to wear blazers with big flowers on my lapel to remind me of joy, all while being classy and showing a wee bit of sass. That's all hard to hide.

If that range doesn't suit someone or their organization then I'm not the person for the position and I'm OK with that.

I'm not anywhere close to a detailed person. I'm the last person you'd want to do your taxes, although we'd have some good laughs and a lot of wine, and I might teach you some new ways to use profanity.

Once I get to know someone, I do use happy faces and exclamation marks in my emails, and my values for both my coaching and health and safety business include fun and joy.

My skirt doesn't twist in quiet rebellion anymore. I am blessed and honoured to work alongside many amazing clients-from doctors, to accountants, to business owners and artists-all becoming more keenly aware of who they are and how they want to show up in the world. That's my joy spot.

The more *Me* I become, the more joy I know.

What hit home for me, even when my skirt being on sideways didn't change me forever, was doing an exercise with my coach where the accountant/lawyer lie smacked me in the face. I knew I wasn't being 100% me, but couldn't put my finger on the real issue.

What I uncovered was that I was trying to be perceived in a certain way and that was all that mattered to me at the time, rather than focusing on being the best version of myself.

I also realized after going over this exercise, that I had made up a story: that goofy people aren't smart or have much to offer. I so often have tried to hide my goofiness in professional settings.

We explored that and she said, "What about Patch Adams? He was smart, and fun, and warm?"

Damn she's good. That hit me like a ton of bricks! I love him. He's goofy, and loving, and smart. I adore him.

My homework was to watch the movie about him and I was choked up the whole time. Patch is crazy, deep, and loved others. He works hard for what matters to him. I can do that. I do that. (If you have not watched this movie, put down this book and go watch it RIGHT NOW! You can thank me later.)

So, now I'm goofy, funny, and serious me. I'm a flower and JoySock wearing girl. I own my own expertise. I do my best to be kind, to honour others with their uniqueness and flavour. I hold space equally for struggle and achievement.

I avoid numbers like the plague, and I am hoping to make the world a better place, just like you, in your own way.

Lay aside what you hope people will perceive you as-if blue suits are your thing-get more. If numbers light you up, BRING THEM ON.

You're here to bring your truth to the world in a way that only you can. That's your joy spot. Let's set the world on fire together with truth, authenticity, and courage.

Reflections

How do you want to be perceived?

How do you not want to be perceived?

How does that hold you back from the truth of who you really are?

When you are tied up by unwanted perceptions, what is the truth of you that others don't get to see?

How can you let more of that true, delicious side of you shine?

For fun, find someone who emulates some of the goodness you have and let them shine a light on your own goodness. Like my Patch Adams. :)

Who is someone you admire, and it feels like they call you to be more yourself?

How would being more you bring you more joy?

Chapter 15 (M/E)

Be Aware

Before we go any further, we're going to need a skill that will help us on our way.

It's mindfulness.

Don't panic, or if you're more like who I used to be, maybe throw up in your mouth just a little when you think of mindfulness.

What does it mean to be mindful? There are many ways to be mindful, but simply put, it's just awareness.

Noticing.

Mindfulness is a skill that allows us to be more aware of what's going on internally and respond to situations rather than unconsciously react.

Seeing as I feel scattered a lot of the time and have issues focusing, you can imagine this slowing down and reflecting doesn't come easy to me and maybe it doesn't to you either.

A while back, I was noticing how I was feeling jealous of people who travelled for spring break; their pics on the beach in the warm sun, taking a break from work-it all made me feel envious. I don't normally feel like this. I normally don't even care. (Precovid when we could actually go somewhere.)

I saw someone walking her dog-she was walking so SLLL-LOOOOOWWWWLY, and I felt irritated. I thought, "Who has time for that?"

My immediate answer, "People who are clearly awesome and perhaps way more evolved than me have time for that."

SHIT! (I warned you, it's not all a bed of roses growing in my mind.)

But it's where my truth lies and if we really want more joy, we need to be aware of what is stealing it, and how we can nurture more of it.

Busyness, discipline, military-style inner voices keep that awareness from coming to the forefront and keep us from living fulfilling lives. They also keep us from joy.

I'm into living life to the fullest and I imagine you are, too. Bring on that goodness!

I used to not know what *play* looked like. The last time I had a desire to play I started a non-profit, and while I love that wee JoySocks baby of mine, it's not so playful as it has grown into toddlerhood, and I'm not about to start another big project. (That "baby" www.joysocks.ca.)

My week was very planned and strategic. One day, I told my daughter that I was having the best day because I was doing laundry during a workday and it was making me very joyful. If laundry is your joy spot, you do you. It is not normally mine.

You guessed it. Her reaction was probably like yours, "LAUNDRY DURING A WORKDAY BROUGHT YOU JOY?!"

Yup, because it was outside of my regularly scheduled events and I felt like a HUGE, and clearly a wee bit lame, non-conformist.

Weekday laundry was great, but seriously, it also felt deeply odd that it made me that happy.

Lately, I feel drawn to not work, to play, to explore, to relax more, and to be a fairy-dust-throwing-love-spreader if I'm to be honest.

I want less routine, I want less rules, I want fewer inner critics who try to convince me that I'll be starving to death by the end of the month if I follow the path of what I long for. That's why I need mindfulness.

Because who are we kidding? These inner voices lie A LOT.

The inner critics tell me that my success will be over by the end of the week. That's never true and I'm drawn constantly to spaciousness. I honour that in extremely specific ways, AND I am committed to avoiding growing more brain tumours, I already have four and that's plenty. I like walks, and short, very timed naps.

I want to notice the small things in life, the little exquisite "beauties" in life-that's where the joy is. Those joy spots are hanging around and I don't want to miss out.

I don't want to be too busy.

I work from home and have become super disciplined in order to do everything I need to get done and to maybe, deep down inside, prove that I am enough. I do it to stop my financial worries that these business-es of mine will dry up and I will be handing out JoySocks and swinging around a pole to pay the bills.

So, I've been trying to implement more mindful moments.

I've been walking away from my office and sitting and drinking my cof-fee without my phone near by-doing nothing, at least for a few minutes.

I was sitting on my porch, feeling the sun on my face, and it felt so deeply delightful, that it choked me up.

The more time I take, the more I feel "feelings" bubbling up.

Some of those feelings aren't so pleasant or pretty, but more often, I feel more joy, and contentment, and goodness.

So, space and more mindfulness are actually doing me good.

I believe that in the stillness of our lives, lies the truth of what we truly want, and what we truly need. I ALSO believe that the universe has a wee bit of weirdness for us all to follow so that we can shine our light in a way that only we can, AND celebrate our own brand of non-conformity, and joyful badassery. We need to be more mindful to do that.

What do you need to slow down, to be in this moment? (You're already doing so well because you're reading this book, my beloved lamb, look at you go!)

When triggers come up, those emotionally charged moments, how can you be more aware, and take a big breath so that you can notice what's going on?

Try this simple exercise. In a mundane moment, notice the wind on your face, your feet on the ground, breathe intentionally for a moment and feel the temperature of the air entering your nose, and when you exhale… this is where the skill is built. See how simple it is?! Your mindfulness is cultivating more space for joy.

Reflections

Any places where you feel resentful and want to switch things up?

What do you need to be more mindful?

How will you become more mindful?

If you allowed more stillness in your life, what might bubble up for you?

What would you do to honour you?

Chapter 16 (M)

Feel It, Free It

Imagine you're holding an orange.

Just an orange.

If you hold an orange in your hand and just "be" with the orange, what do you see? Smell? Feel? I know, look at you. You are being so mindful.

An orange. That's it.

We rarely allow ourselves to just be in any moment. Even now, besides reading these words, where else is your brain? Are you thinking about your next client? Your grocery list? Or perhaps your next spreadsheet? (Heaven help you.)

And so, what do we do when we experience challenging emotions? Perhaps stressing about those spreadsheets, or a tough conversation we just had.

We let our brain take off like a jet engine with interpretations about those emotions and thinking about the various outcomes to the scenario that caused the stress in the first place. Maybe we worry about something that could happen, or why something is happening, or that someone is mad or disappointed in us for a small mistake. That's what we DO.

What does that cost us?

A lot.

A while back, it was my first full day that I had appointments and meetings after my vacation. I woke up with some apprehension about getting back into the real work-swing of things.

I felt a sense of dread. Within a millisecond I heard the inner "beat-up-brute" inside my head say, *of course, you feel this, you're a lazy $&#*!*

Wow, she's a little harsh, but she must be cute because I kept her around.

This is the hard bit of mindfulness; you get to see what's actually going on in your head. I recognized the voice because I was practicing being more aware. However, that didn't mean I was immune to the messages.

I had another voice saying, "You don't like to work," as well as a chorus of catastrophe chiming in less than lovingly, "How are you even going to keep your head above water? It'd be a miracle if you have any clients soon."

Then, thoughts of being impoverished and trying to find work flooded my brain and the idea of my back-up plan of swinging around a pole to make a living if things get really bad came up. Just wait for it-Leona becomes a pole dancer. (Well that's an entire other chapter and if I become a pole dancer, I'll leave that for another book.)

This shit storm doesn't happen over 20 minutes-this is all in a matter of one second. I'm that good.

Maybe I'm the only one who has a feeling, and then interprets that feeling, and then catastrophizes, but I don't think so. Science confirms that we all do it. Sorry to not be able to leave you out of this mess.

What does this have to do with the orange?

It has EVERYTHING to do with the orange.

The orange is a form of mindfulness. We experience the orange in a moment, as it is, a round piece of orange-coloured fruit. We don't usually think of the orange squirting us in the eye, we don't think of it rotting in a week, or what it will smell like at that point. We allow ourselves to experience the orange, in its original state, in that moment.

If we experience an emotion, especially a tough one, be with it with curiosity. Stay with it. Don't pile on a freight train full of thoughts and interpretations. Things become so much easier when we can notice our emotions without judgment.

The brutal thoughts I had about how lazy I was for not wanting to go back to work stayed with me for the better part of that morning.

What started with a wee bit of dread over going back to work, had smeared my brain with self doubt and, frankly, crap.

What's the alternative?

We can get curious and simply notice, and acknowledge, what we're feeling. I was feeling dread, anxiety, and some apprehension. There, that's not so bad.

When we recognize we are feeling an emotion, and get curious as to what that emotion is, we drop the charge of that emotion by about 25 per cent by naming it. That's a great deal!

You don't have to say the emotion out loud, but think, *I feel...* and name the emotion.

Try not to make statements like, "I am..." as in "I am terrified."

Your brain over identifies with the "I am" statements and we don't want that. It's an emotion, you are feeling it, it has not become you.

Then you can observe the thoughts that are associated with that feeling as simple awareness.

OK, now for the good stuff. When you're feeling emotions that you like, savour them. Relish the feelings and think of how great that feels. Take time to notice what they feel like in your body. This creates new pathways in your brain, neural pathways, so your brain is primed and ready to seek out, and feel those feelings more deeply. YUM! Feel your joy spots getting bigger? They are and you're becoming more emotionally intelligent. You're so delightful!

Reflections

Think of a tough situation that you have been in recently. What emotions did you experience? You can experience a number of emotions at once, and the more accurate you are at identifying them, the quicker you will feel their charge lessen.

Be mindful, what are you feeling right now? Take time throughout the day to slow down, and recognize the emotion that you're feeling.

1. Notice the feeling or sensation, observe it like the orange.

2. Don't judge it—it's a feeling. Like the orange, it has every right to be what it is, and it will change.

3. Realize that whatever emotion you're feeling, it's NORMAL-there are no right or wrong feelings.

Chapter 17 (M)

How Well Do You Surf?

I bet you're a much better surfer than you know.

How often do your thoughts surf into the future? How often do you future surf?

Future surfing starts with *what if*.

What if I lose my job?

What if I get a terminal diagnosis?

What if…

My coach called the *what ifs* Future Surfing.

She said if we are asking what if, we are not present, and the present is all we have. She had fourth stage cancer, so she was in the know.

What if this doesn't work out?

What if something happens to my child?

What ifs are joy killers and worry steroid injectors.

If you're a good ole regular person, chances are that these *what ifs* are feeding a good deal of what you're thinking.

I wrote a blog about balancing pain and joy when I was diagnosed with a pancreatic tumour at the same time as celebrating a tumour that had disappeared, when I was asked by a friend how one *does* both. I sat with that for a bit and came up with an answer.

I decided to invite the pain of the worry into my current joy.

As weird as it may sound, it wasn't so hard.

I thought, after the shock wore off of my newly diagnosed tumour, that I was not any different than I was before the knowledge of it. I felt the same. I had no pain, no issues, or awareness of its presence.

A few days after the dreaded phone call from my doc, I was at boot camp and doing burpees and push-ups from my toes, which felt amazing as I was no spring chicken. At that point, I had no injuries and could do anything I wanted.

I was 48 years old.

The average life expectancy for a woman with my condition is 48.4 years. This is awesome as I'm planning to at least double that; cognitively clear and diaper free. (If you're certain about what you want, I figured you might as well be specific too!)

I thought, "Why am I stealing the joy I feel today about being so healthy, by worrying about the results of my upcoming tests to figure out more about the tumour?"

Pain comes when I lived in the *what ifs*.

I didn't want to surf. Heck, it didn't even appeal to me on beach vacations because I'd always think, what if I get eaten by a shark? I can literally hear the *Jaws* soundtrack just thinking about it. You can see how intense this surfing thing can be for me.

What if…

What if it is cancer?

What if I do need to have my pancreas removed?

What if I become a diabetic? (Which is what happens when you remove your pancreas.)

What if this is the beginning of the end?

And the bare bones truth of this was: this was the beginning of the end.

This was also a new day, AND a new opportunity to really live. And an opportunity to live with purpose, and meaning, and to find the joy sprinkled in each day.

I do not want to miss out on this day and its beauty because of my surfing into the future.

I want today. I want to squeeze all the delicious life juice that's here today. I want to burpee joyfully. I want to connect with people with intention. I want to spread the good news that each of us is here for a reason, to support people as they tap into that reason, and help others find greater meaning and joy.

I'm ditching the *what if* surfboard. I purposefully set it up against the wall and when it topples over on me, creating uncertainty, and fear that sucks the very essence out of me, I will choose gratitude in that moment, whatever that might be, to come back to the present.

Today, at this very moment, I am comfortably sitting on a couch, with a new computer on my lap (what a blessing), in a comfy robe, with a furnace pumping warm air into my office, and I am writing this in an amazing body, that is digesting my fave source of liquid love (coffee) and I have EVERYTHING I need. Right now.

This moment is such a gift.

For this present of presence, my heart sings with gratitude.

May yours as well.

Reflections

Where are you Future Surfing?

What are the *what ifs* that have you tethered to your surfboard?

Who would you be if you had nothing to worry about?

What do you notice right now in this moment? What does your body feel like? The temperature of the room? How's your heart right now?

What are you grateful for right now? Being aware of that helps you to stay present.

Look at you go with this mindfulness! ;)

Chapter 18 (P)

Who Would You Be?

Who would you be if you worried less?

I'd be free. I'd be liberated. I would do things differently. I'd run my businesses differently. I'd spend more money, probably have more fun, and I would start shouting from the mountain tops that life is precious and we should all get out and squeeze all the joy juice out of it.

What do you worry about?

For me, I worry about one thing the most-money. When I think about my health, it's not so much the treatment, or complications I might encounter as a result of my genetic condition. I worry about not being able to work. That's my BIG worry.

I always tell my son, who has already had brain surgery (a veteran), that I have no time for tumours, and he always reminds me that I do have time, and I'll be fine taking some time off.

You'd think that if I am worried about money that I must be scraping the bottom of the financial barrel. I'm not. Someone last week said that if they had my condition they would be planning like crazy. I have in some sense, but just around money. I have saved enough that I could take at least a quarter of a year off.

Worry makes me feel like I did when I had an "eating thing." (I have not been officially diagnosed with an eating disorder, so I call it a "thing.") I would weigh myself all the time and if I weighed less, I would eat less to keep the loss going. If I weighed more, I would eat less to make sure that it shifted things.

It was an awful feeling. I felt out of control. I had to get rid of my scale and trust myself that I would find the balance without checking constantly. I react similarly with money, and it seems like when I have more money, I save more money-not loosen the reins. Not logical. When I have less, I save more again. Like the eating thing.

So, why am I so worried about money? There's nothing to worry about, right?

Wrong-worry is worry. Worry is a reaction to anxiety, and it's not necessarily logical. Some people worry about safety. I hear fellow moms worry about their kids going to clubs, about their kids being drugged, about getting home safe, about Uber rides. They worry about all the kid things.

I'm not heartless but I don't worry about any of that. At all. My kids have never even had a curfew. I sleep like a baby and never worry about them despite hearing their drunken tales, though I do wonder how they even remember their addresses to tell the Uber driver (perhaps they're talented ;).

I feel vulnerable even talking about my worry. In my family, my mom modelled and told us very clearly that you don't worry. She didn't worry. She had 10 brain surgeries in 25 years and she really didn't seem to stress. She modelled to keep moving, be grateful for everything, and go on.

I'm a wee bit sick of my worries, and as a coach who is committed to helping my clients work through their challenges, I am even more committed to working through my "stuff." That's integrity to me.

Sometimes, I ask myself questions that I would normally ask my clients. The following helped me a TONNE.

Question: What do you worry about?

My answer: Money.

Question: What's underneath that worry?

My answer: Safety (basic need), independence (I have avoided leaning on other people), resourcefulness (I love to save, don't love to spend unless it's super delightful, and even then it's probably on sale).

Also, there are messages like, "You need to pull your own weight. You need to be responsible. You're not enough (not prepared enough, not strong enough to manage all this)." Yuck. Those buggers run around in my brain.

Question: What behaviours does that trigger?

My answer: I save even more, "batten down the hatches," and find ways to save money everywhere, AND check my bank account often to increase a feeling of control. Sometimes I check my account without realizing I'm worried. This is when I know I need to look at what's going on.

Sometimes, I'm stressed about other stuff and I'm checking on money things as a way of transferring the worry to my old money go-to.

Question: How do I know when I'm living in the trigger and not the truth?

My answer: I am saving on crazy things, and my joy is depleted because I'm not present. I'm scouring for ways to live scarcely. I am tempted to check my bank accounts even when I know exactly how much is in there.

Question: What supports me to live in the truth and not the worry?

My answer: Look at my history. I have never been without a roof over my head or without money. TRUST: I have never not had what I needed. Never.

Tap into my truth statement that I use when things feel out of control: "I always have what I need, when I need it."

I used to believe the lie that I needed to see it all now. I don't.

Question: What behaviours support the truth?

My answer: Keeping healthy, move my body, have good relationships, meditation/prayer, sleep, naps, being creative, and talking with a trusted friend about my fears and shame regarding feeling not enough, or successful enough. I also don't check my bank balance more than once a week.

Lastly, and this is where we spark some joy (at least I do), change your thinking about your worry into gratitude. I stop and think how grateful I am every time I pay a bill with ease. I am thankful every time I bring home a huge load of groceries. I am thankful when I recall I have no debt outside of my mortgage. I can feel the joy increasing and a joy spot forming on the horizon of my worry.

We all worry, and our worries won't ever all go away entirely, but we are also meant to live, really live, and not be living in the scarcity of the messages that our worries feed.

We ARE meant to live in the abundance of joy. Life is stressful enough; we don't need to be hijacked by the lies that worry spits at us.

Reflections

Think of something you worry about.

Give yourself permission to explore it. Worry doesn't have to be logical. This is a form of mindfulness.

Answering the following questions:
What am I worrying about?

What's underneath that worry?

What behaviours does that trigger? Sometimes we live such triggered lives that we don't know what's making us do certain things.

How do I know when I'm living in the trigger and not the truth?

What supports me to live in the truth and not the worry?

What behaviours support the truth?

What could you be grateful for around the things you normally worry about?

Chapter 19 (P/M)

You Can Still Squat(ish)

I wake up to turn off my alarm, and get up for boot camp and, as I roll over, I feel this excruciating pain tear through my upper back. I literally cannot move. My first thought is, "What's going on?"

My next thought is, "What's happening to me?"

Before I go any further, I will add a disclaimer. We all see those *NSFW* warnings when a post on social media is going to show some nudity and it's not safe to watch at work. The warning on this chapter might fall under *FFCPEW*: Full Frontal Crazy Person Exposure Warning (no nudity, don't panic), but for now I will call it *FFVW*: Full Frontal Vulnerability Warning.

I am a certified facilitator in the *Daring Way*, based on the research of Brené Brown. Part of her work in her book *Rising Strong* and supporting curriculum, is about slowing down the process of feeling things, then thinking, and then doing things based on the interpretation.

Her work has transformed my life and work like no other has, and because of that, I am able to slow down, and be very aware of what is going on for me. Which can be embarrassing.

As I'm lying in bed, the thoughts going through my head are:

Get out of bed, you can still go to boot camp.

But I can't even move.

You can roll out and still do squats, even if your arms don't move.

What if this keeps going on? I will get fat. (Insert mental pic of me in a fat suit.)

Slow down, you're OK.

I'm not OK, I can barely breathe, I can't move, AND I'm in the worst pain ever.

Then the medical/logical(ish) Leona steps in. (Dang I am "gifted" and, I imagine, based on the research you are, too. ;)

Could your spinal tumour have burst? Oh gosh, can that happen? Where are my two tumours? Damn it! L-something, T-something? Is this the L-section of my back? Where is it on the L?

I decide I need to find my latest MRI and look, but I still can't move so that's not going to work.

Of course, you don't know where it is, I think. *You don't do details and you're so disorganized.*

Shame is a sneaky bastard and likes to slink in when we feel vulnerable.

Crap! I knew this lack of attention to detail would come back to haunt me at the worst time.

The pain starts moving between my shoulder blades and radiates down one arm.

Could you be having a heart attack? I am having trouble breathing, but only because of the pain.

I continue.

Is my skin a weird colour?

I can't move so I think, "It doesn't feel like it's a weird colour." (Just an FYI-you can't feel whether your skin is a funny colour, but I was nevertheless reassured that I must look normal.) I should tell you that I taught first aid for 15 years for the Red Cross and this is still the crap I come up with.

After five minutes of trying to get out of bed, I finally manage it. Yes!

I'm covered in sweat and so nauseous from the pain that I think, "I'm going to faint." (And throw up on the carpet as I can't move, even though I'm now standing-my morning squat option fading further into the background.)

I lie back onto the end of my bed. By this time, I have horrible tunnel vision and a very loud sound booming in my ears. It sounds like an airplane taking off two feet from my head. This is what one does right before fainting. My only accurate thought in all of this is to follow up with something more dramatic.

With the vision issue (and a clearly rapidly approaching state of psychosis), I think, "Shit, I can't see, I'm about to barf, and that noise won't go away. I'm having a stroke."

I've taught first aid for a long time. I know my medical emergencies. I'm also worried that I will have to call 911, but I can't even move to call. I rule out the stroke idea. I'm not having a stroke, as back pain is not listed as one of the onset symptoms. Phew!

In a few minutes, the nausea, blackness, and ear ringing subside, and I slowly get up.

I have a moment of clarity and text my kiddo that I won't be getting up as I'm not feeling well (AKA dying on the bed, having a stroke/heart attack/tumour bursting panic attack), so I write, "I'm sorry, I won't be making you a latte this morning." Moms do these things while we are dying. I have no idea why.

My next "sane" thought, "How will I make coffee? I can't move, and I SURELY won't be able to twist open my stove top espresso maker."

Let's be clear about one thing-coffee is my life force. It is like mother's milk.

More panic sets in.

It's only 6 a.m., and I'm leading a workshop this morning based on *The Gifts of Imperfection* by Brené Brown (is there irony here or what?).

How will I set up or be able to breathe while I talk? For the third time in 20 years, I have to take a day off work.

I DON'T TAKE DAYS OFF WORK!

But I am today.

I'm a mess-are you picking up on that yet?

Are you sensing some deep-seated issues? Awareness can bring up A LOT of that!

I manage to push through the WORST pain (I've experienced natural childbirth, lest one thinks I have no reference to extraordinary pain-9 lb babe pain), to take some ibuprofen and lay back down, praying the medication helps a wee, tiny bit.

I wait for an hour, telling myself, "Go to sleep, be kind to yourself."

Then, knowing that I can't even take a full breath without stabbing pain, I lie on the bed to take stock of even more of my thoughts, some of which include: *You're a wimp, it's just your back, you're fine, just roll over, and get moving-you're very healthy, and strong, this is ridiculous.* (I finally abandon the thought that I could do any squats at this point-a small bit of reality-based wisdom. :)

I continue with, *you're not very kind to yourself at all, listen to your self talk, and how is it that you lead these workshops, and here you are literally whipping yourself? You suck at self-compassion!*

Here's the truth. I tell people all the time that we are a beautiful mess-we are all a combo of darkness and light. I am that mess.

Being physically incapacitated is a VERY vulnerable and a huge trigger for me. That emotion, vulnerability, sets me off. I was not modelled self care in times of sickness. We were taught to always keep moving. (I know you know this. ;)

As I mentioned earlier, my mom had an aneurysm, a bleed in her head, when I was 16. She told my dad she needed to go to the hospital as she could barely move, or see, but told him she would make us lunch before she left. We were teenagers, AKA, we could feed ourselves. She almost died from that bleed, and yet she made us lunch. That's insane (love her, but that's nuts).

WHO DOES THIS?

We do this, I do this-to keep hidden, to avoid feeling vulnerable, to buck up, and not ask for help…

After I get up, I am able to move a bit better. I can lift one arm to warm up the coffee my son had left behind (funny how people bless you if you let them).

The movement seems to help me feel more alive (and worthy, if you want to know the bare butt-naked truth of it all).

I start to empty the dishwasher with the one arm that moves, and time my breathing that is also still ridiculously hard. At the same time, my daughter can hear the utensils moving.

She yells from her room, "STOP EMPTYING THE DISHWASH-ER MOM. BE LAZY!!"

I yell back, "I CAN'T BE LAZY. I DON'T DO LAZY. THAT'S MY PROBLEM!"

It's so eye-opening to proclaim your pathology to the world.

I am letting you in on this in a hope that I'm not stand-alone-crazy, and that I'm not alone. That there may be triggers for you that bring out the mess in you, so that we can rumble with this madness together.

The truth is, until I'm physically stopped in my tracks, I don't know this messy part of myself so well until I'm in it. I have laughed about that part of me, but that day it smacked me between the eyeballs.

It made me realize that I try to run away from discomfort, but the healing is found in leaning in, and "relaxing" into the pain, breathing deeply, even when it hurts to do so.

By getting curious about what I am feeling, and thinking in those moments, I can understand what's really going on, and reflect on the physical sensations and emotions needing to be honoured.

I become more aware of what my triggers are and how I can be kind to myself and, furthermore, let others be kind to me.

Why is it that I can relax when it's on my terms and not when I'm forced to?

We so need to focus on what we can do, not what we can't.

Dropping into gratitude for anything good in those moments grounds me and helps me so much to reduce stress, and be more mindful. I hear my super busy kiddo emptying the dishwasher as my honey is trying to ease the knots out of my back, such simultaneous goodness.

Laughing always helps me, too. After my *collapse-am I having a stroke? moment*, I peeled myself off the bed and saw a book lying nearby called *When the Body Says No* by Gabor Maté. I had to laugh as the universe blew me a divine kiss, and perhaps, gave me a wee wink. When the body says no-really?! OK, I get it, sometimes it's all too hilarious.

I have to trust that whatever I am going through it will pass, maybe not quickly or perhaps maybe never completely, but I will find a new way of being.

I'm a recovering human *doer*. I am learning to be a better human *being*, loved by myself and others, for the beautiful intricate mess that I am.

Brené Brown, my beloved soul sister, whispered in my ear, and reminded me of what I was going to talk about with my group that morning as I recovered enough to lead the session. Well-ish. I still have a long way to go with the human doer syndrome.

"Cultivating the courage, compassion, and connection to wake up in the morning and think, no matter what gets done today, I am enough. It's going to bed at night thinking Yes, I am imperfect and vulnerable and sometimes afraid, but that doesn't change the truth that I am also brave and worthy of love and belonging."

(Brené Brown, *The Gifts of Imperfection*)

Reflections

What experiences do you have trouble being with? Maybe it's sickness, conflict, not being perfect…

What thoughts go through your head when you get sidelined by a wall that life drops in your path?

What makes these spaces easier for you?

Thank you for joining me on this messy ride of life. I am honoured to be here, super-blessed to be able to sit, and write about this. To everyone, all of us, who struggle-I salute you.

So, let's continue on this messy and delicious journey.

You might be wondering what does all of this have to do with joy? If we don't know what's taking us away from joy, we can't create more of it, so this is the work of cultivating more of it.

Chapter 20 (M)

What Do You Do When It All Goes Wrong?

Everything is going to crap. What do you do?

Freak out!

Clearly, that's always my first and most obvious go-to choice. (No surprises based on what I just wrote in the previous chapter. Sorry folks!)

When that's not an option, go for the second option, and give into what is actually happening. I rarely, if ever, choose that option.

Third option: keep forging ahead-awesome option! ALWAYS! (Not.) I KNOW I AM A SLLLOOOOOOOOWWWW LEARNER.

You too?

Bear with me.

Here's a glimpse of another time…to show that I am actually trying to change, just like you. I just need a few tries. :)

I'm lying in bed early one Friday morning and I have this weird pain. It is different from the pain that had stopped me from going to boot camp. This pain is just under my ribs on my left side. Perhaps I am a collector of weird pains (does this stuff happen to you?!). The pain comes like contractions and I sleep in between them, or at least rest. I have a tumour on my pancreas, and I am a wee bit concerned that it may be acting up, even though, at that moment, I have no idea what side of me my pancreas is located on and what the symptoms of said tumour would be.

Things get worse.

I could care less about what's causing this because within an hour I have ALL the symptoms of the stomach flu, including fever and aches. Normally, this is an unpleasant experience to say the least, but you take the day off work, take meds and all is well. I'll spare you the gory details, but suffice to say, I am nearly dying and going from both ends. I hate the stomach flu more than anything.

Later that day, I have to lead a workshop for the entire evening, and the entire next day. This had been in the works for the past three months, with almost 20 people signed up AND IT WAS IN ANOTHER CITY.

Three hours away (insert *Jaws* soundtrack here).

I can't be away from a bathroom for more than a few minutes at a time, making the drive seem like a flat-out impossibility.

To make matters worse, throwing up makes me miss my mom-I hate that. When I get the flu, I miss her, desperately so.

The story of my life has always been that I have trouble asking for help…in every single area of my life. I am working on this.

I have to reach out because of sheer desperation, and I text my beloved. He brings over flowers and meds. Having someone take care of me always helps ease the momma-ache (he didn't show up in a Hazmat suit like I would have either, which I think is extra thoughtful).

I email the workshop organizer at 5:30 a.m. that I am in dire straights. I know there's nothing worse than having someone cancel at noon when they've been sick since the morning, and you had no idea. So, I email her right away. I scramble to find a sub for the workshop, which doesn't amount to anything.

I take meds-tonnes of them. Enough to bung up an elephant.

I pace myself as I try to get ready. By 11 a.m., I can move, and the meds are helping with the symptoms, and I take one-hour naps between showering, putting on makeup, and getting dressed.

I don't die in the process, which is my current success marker. Sometimes you have to aim low.

I decide to go to the workshop, relieving the organizers and, in a way, myself. I can't even carry my workshop/overnight bag to the car as I am so weak and worried that any strain will undo the mercy of the meds I've been freebasing.

I lead the workshop-three hours on Friday evening and eight hours on Saturday. I can hardly eat, and I am popping my array of pills to manage.

As I finish the workshop and make the two-and-a-half-hour drive back to my house (I gave myself permission to speed. I would show the police officer my permission slip if I got pulled over and my half empty bottle of Pepto-Bismol :) and crawl into bed, only to feel sick again for a good portion of the night.

I was talking to a doctor after this and he said one of the biggest challenges that sick people face is giving themselves permission to go home and be sick. That made me feel moderately normal.

He said so many people fight their illnesses rather than giving themselves what they need. We talked about people working through chemotherapy and not taking the rest, and seeming proud of it. I did think that I could be one of those people who don't stop to listen for even half a second to what their body needs…

What was my big lesson in all of this? (And finally, a glimpse of me learning-PHEW!)

DON'T EVER DO THIS!

Don't do what I did.

I didn't want to live this way anymore. I was tired of pushing, and striving, and dragging myself around. It's a symptom of not wanting to let people down, trying to be tough, and strong. It is knowing in your head that it's all too much, and soldiering on anyways.

I needed a reminder to slow down and honour my body, and my sickness. Not keep going.

I know it's hard…IT'S RIDICULOUSLY HARD.

Some might say, "Nice for you to take time off, but I need the money." Or,

"Handy for you, you've clearly got some sick days, days off in lieu, some disability, some sugar daddy."

Nope, none of those. At the time, I was a self-employed single mom, but when I really think of what I count as wealth, it includes time and health. Running myself ragged is not what I really want.

I want lots of time on this planet, and I want to be healthy enough to fill that time well.

How am I going to do that?

I don't have all the answers or the five-point plan to make all of this unfold with ease. All I know is that I want to listen more intently to my body and what it needs. I don't want to detach my head from it and drag it around against its will.

I want a life filled with richness, and wealth; time, and health to enjoy all the goodness that this life has to offer.

Above the noise of demands and pressure, I will listen and try to respond gently to what my body needs.

Are you listening to what you really need? I'm trying!

Reflections

When you listen gently to your body, what is it that it wants more of?

What does it want less of?

What's one thing you'd like to do on a daily basis to listen to and honour your body?

Let's move forward and gather up more joy, but let's look into more of the shadows first. Don't worry, we'll hold hands.

Chapter 21 (P)

The Joy Ride

It wasn't your average joy ride. It felt more like a roller coaster, strapped in and with g-forces on the turns and dives that would snap your head back. It was a ride through the illness of a child and one that taught me so much.

We got up at 4:30 a.m., and as I sat next to my 18-year-old son in the car, I felt like I was bringing a soldier to war.

He was quiet and determined as we arrived at the hospital and I felt an overwhelming weight on my shoulders as they prepped him for brain surgery. I could do nothing to help him. He was truly a soldier-calm, stoic, brave and true to who he is: kind and courageous.

He was having a dangerously located brain tumour removed. It wasn't a random one. He bore not only his own worries but the weight of our family history. He'd lost his grandmother well before his birth to the same kind of tumour and an uncle who has suffered greatly from many of the same surgeries and been left with physical challenges because of them.

My son was totally aware that not everyone came out "OK" after that kind of operation and not everyone even makes it.

As we waited for him to be rolled into the surgical suite, he asked me to take a picture of his "virgin" head, scar free and whole, knowing it would never be the same and it would bear the mark of his suffering and, ultimately, his healing.

A beautiful older male nurse asked if we had any questions and looked at my son's father and me with such loving intensity. The nurse said, "Don't worry, we will take good care of your boy."

His gaze gave me strength and I felt a divine brush from his reassuring words.

We said goodbye to our beloved boy, our man-child, our deeply courageous soldier.

Where was the joy in this ride?

It was there, like little lights in the darkness, bringing with it brief bright patches.

Our family was surrounded by loved ones who came from all over to help us pass the time as the surgery took place. Like doulas, our family and friends helped us in what otherwise would have been a slow, anguishing journey.

It takes courage to walk alongside those who suffer, yet they showed up; drove from hours away to stand alongside us in our angst and to silently be with us.

There was joy in that support.

Like quiet sparks of joy, knowing we were not alone; we were loved, and we were held in a divine grace that walked alongside us in the most troubled times.

A nurse came down every 90 minutes after peeking in on the surgery to tell us that my son was doing OK. My baby, with his head cracked open, was more vulnerable than most have ever been.

There was hint of joy in the updates.

When the surgeon called to say my son was doing well; and he might have some trouble with balance and walking but he was "well."

There was joy in those words. My son was OK, that was all that mattered.

When we got to see him right after surgery, his suffering was more than I could bear. I well up right now just thinking of his anguish and of watching the nurse doing whatever we asked to ease my boy's pain.

There was joy in her willingness.

Not the kind of joy that makes you jump up and down, like you've won the lottery, but a deep gratitude for small mercies. Small graces that make the most intolerable situations more tolerable.

Joy has different faces and when we know those different aspects of joy, we notice it more often.

When, after a brutal night of inadequate pain meds, the medical team stepped in to alleviate his pain and he slept, a nurse clapped her hands and jumped up and down.

There was joy in her jumping. (I love her!)

When he got up and walked, albeit wobbly, two days after the surgery, there was joy.

Joy is different than happiness although they are closely related. Joy contains an aspect of happiness, but it is more deeply rooted; rooted in the good earthy, visceral goodness that is available to all of us despite tragedy and pain. We just need to be willing to notice it.

It's the hand on your shoulder that says, "I'm here with you."

It's fruit that your friend brings to the hospital and when you put it in your mouth you feel a burst of delight.

Joy doesn't fix things or change the fact that you ate that fruit as you held your loved one's hand while he was in a hospital bed, but it is the lubrication that keeps us moving on the hardest of days and we miss out on it if we aren't present to its fleeting touch.

There was joy watching my son navigate stairs and doing it without the help of the cane that was needed earlier in his recovery. There is pain in healing, but so much joy in the little miracles along the way.

Years have passed since this ride began, since the day that scarred not only him, but all of us in a way. There has been joy on this roller coaster ride that is more profoundly and deeply felt than I've ever known.

I would not ask for suffering like that again but if it does present itself, I trust that there will be joy spots there to give me enough of its elixir to keep moving and trusting, even on the most difficult of days.

Joy is not the absence of pain-there will always be pain and stress. Joy does become more readily available when we lean into the pain and feel all that we feel. Pain, when we wrestle with it and feel all that it brings, burrows valleys in our hearts; deep crevices that are capable of producing wellsprings of joy.

When we avoid or numb out pain and the emotions that we are less comfortable with, we also numb and lessen the capacity we have for the emotions we long for like love, happiness, and joy. In a way, pain can serve us and does carve out more room for joy.

Joy-it's not here just for me, or for a fortunate few, it's here for you, too. The world is hungry for more of it and it is available for all of us.

It may be lingering in the corners of our lives, but it's there. It requires presence and gratitude to lock it in more deeply.

Will you create space for it, even when you are caught up in the darkness of pain?

Joy may be all we have to inject the wee bit of strength we need to keep moving forward. My wish for you today, and everyday, is that you will see it, feel it, and know it, and that somehow the miracle of joy will light your path on the darkest of days.

Lean into the pain you might be experiencing, give yourself permission to feel all those feelings and also take the time to notice where joy shows up too. It makes the burden lighter.

Reflections

Reflect on a difficult time. Recall the situation, the anguish, the loss. Take the time to reflect on all of it, and also look for the spots of joy that you experienced during that time.

Was there anything, or anyone, who helped ease the pain or let the light in, even for a brief moment, during that time?

Savour all of it; the hard times that you persevered through and the little spaces where grace carried you.

Chapter 22 (P/M)

THIS SUCKS!!!

Seriously sucks!

That was my first thought as I rolled out of bed. My son had just had brain surgery the day before and I was exposed to suffering like I had never witnessed. I was exhausted. It was such a hard time.

We don't have to be going through anything life-threatening to feel overwhelmed and out of control. Life can be so stressful.

Deadlines at work, childcare issues, sick parents, struggling in a relationship – those are just a few of the situations that make us feel like we're drowning.

We all have our own *stresscipes* – those ingredients in life that, when combined, make us feel like we are living on the edge, stressed out and overwhelmed.

Suffering can be so isolating, you can't really carry another's pain and nothing anyone does gives you a break from your own.

I reflected on what the key pieces are that do lighten the load.

Here are some of the key skills to managing in rough times:

1. Surround yourself with supportive people.

These people are the ones who are really there for you. They know how to be empathic and support you the way that works for you-no drama, no agenda.

I knew my son's surgery would be long and very stressful, I knew I needed people with me to pass the time so I planned to be at the hospital and plant myself in a location where friends and relatives could come and go. One of my friends even brought a charcuterie plate-my actual love language on a platter (no wine, sadly). So good on a day you think you won't be able to eat a thing but need to more than ever.

2. Ask for what you need and want.

This is way harder than it sounds. When you're in a very stressful situation, it's hard to even think straight.

Keep asking yourself,

"What do I want?"

"What do I need?"

It sounds so basic. Listen to your gut response. Maybe you need a rest and, if that's not an option, even a break might help-follow that.

At one point, I couldn't even think, and I enlisted one of my people to help me make decisions about even small things, which seemed impossible at the time. They decided what we would have for dinner. That saved my life.

3. Be flexible.

What helps you one day, may not be helpful the next-that's OK. Life is messy and there's no perfect road map to manoeuvre through all the crap sometimes. Go with the flow.

4. Be Intentional.

Notice what you say to yourself. Yes, you will think you can't do this, this sucks and YES IT DOES! You may be in the thick of it and have no choice but to soldier on. When this happens, do things that make you feel better and think more positively. There's a reason we send flowers to people, it brightens things up. Tell yourself things that are supportive, "This will get better."

"I can do this."

Be intentional and go out of your way to greet others, say good morning, give a sincere thank you, authentically compliment someone. This gets us out of our own heads and blesses another.

No surprise but I wore goofy socks everyday to the hospital and one day someone commented on them and I said, "I felt like dressing for a funeral today but I chose to dress in these to help me."

Socks, clothes, whatever it is that helps you feel better, do it. That intention can go a long way.

5. Be present.

Stress can be overwhelming. Watch for future surfing; any statement that starts with *what if*, can be terrifying.

"What if this gets worse?"

You know that voice that wreaks havoc with your mind, it's so rarely positive and the truth is, you don't know. Do what you can to stay centred and not go there. I always tell myself to be where my feet are. Not a moment ahead or a moment behind.

Any questions that start with *why* are also not helpful at this moment because you don't have the capacity to explore that. Save that for a session with a coach or therapist.

Like I said, I remind myself to "be where my feet are."

I am in the hospital, I am drinking coffee, I am comforting a sick kiddo…Being present reduces stress and helps us to simply be with what is.

6. Be kind to yourself.

Your situation feels like hell. Don't beat yourself up for not doing things the way you'd hoped, or for not reacting or being as engaged and energized as you'd like to be. Speak to yourself like you would a friend, with compassion and kindness. You're doing the best you can.

On the morning of the fifth day after the surgery, my son said, "Today I am going to choose to be more positive than yesterday." I loved that and it helped me make the same choice. The kid couldn't even sit up two days before that.

This isn't candy coating our feelings, but it does mean we make a choice about how we interact with our circumstances and we choose what serves us.

The other must haves were a huge bar of dark chocolate that I carried everywhere and shared like a communion wafer with anyone who was with me. I also had a gorgeous glass of wine at the end of the day, long hugs, good coffee, and I took the stairs instead of the elevator. The smallest things can bring the greatest joy.

What does support look like for you when you're struggling?

Reflections

Who are the people you need right now?

What will you ask from them?

Is there anyone who you don't need around you right now?

Put up some boundaries. Decide what's OK and communicate clearly around what's not.

Ask yourself and act with the answers that come up:

What do I want?

What do I need?

What can you be more flexible about right now?

How can you be more intentional right now with your words, surroundings, and actions?

How can you be more present?

Write down what you are thinking, feeling, and noticing in this moment without any judgment.

What would you say to a friend who is suffering?

If you were being compassionate with yourself, what would you say to yourself?

What would you like to stop saying to yourself?

Chapter 23 (M)

They're In His Eyes

"They're in his eyes," the ophthalmologist says as she examines my son's eyes.

"They're what?" I ask.

"He has tumours in his eyes."

I'd just finished telling the doctor that my mom had been blind in one eye from the medical condition that she and I share with my son. But I didn't think he'd get eye tumours.

Until now.

The first thing that goes through my mind is, *oh god, why not me?*

The genetic disorder that three generations of my family share means we are missing a tumour suppressor gene. We are at high risk to grow tumours in 10 places in our bodies, some are cancerous and some benign. All can cause serious issues.

So far, my son and I both have brain tumours; I have spinal tumours. My eyes were checked just before him and I was fine.

Why not me?

I am his mom. I'm sitting here with my pupils dilated and I miss the bullet and he gets three: one tumour in one eye and two in the other.

How do we navigate through these tough times without being bowled over?

I want to start by saying I think I have an amazing life. I am very blessed. But this is crap and I'm not happy about how things are going.

I don't, however, hate my condition. You see it on social media, "F#$& cancer!"

Some people say that when they have been impacted by a certain disease. This condition, for one thing, is on every strand of my DNA and my son's and I love every bit if his DNA and I'm learning to love mine. So, I can't hate this condition.

Plus, some of the tools I've learned to deal with all of this are so helpful when life lobs another bit of crap my way.

Someone asked me how I do manage everything around this disease without getting depressed.

I do feel down, and I do feel sad, but I don't let those feelings take over any more than I let joy or happiness rose colour things.

First of all, I try to feel the feels, all of them, however hard they might be.

I feel so guilty that it's my son and not me who has these tumours. I feel guilty and I hold that emotion apart from me. I feel it, logical or not. It is a feeling and it's worthy of time and space and I don't over identify with it. It's like holding out the orange. I am not the orange nor the feeling.

I tell someone how I feel.

These people are those whom I trust with my soul. That means they will hold the space that I need to be me, whatever that looks like. That includes me feeling guilty, sad, or laughing that my pupils look like I did a line of cocaine because they are still dilated from my eye exam. My people love me, and I trust them. They do not candy coat any of this and they do not try to make any of this better. They empathize. That helps.

I try to stay in the moment and be mindful.

I live where my feet are, just like the chapter on future surfing, I can't *future surf* to what could happen. It could be good or bad and rarely do we go to the happiest of endings. So, I don't go anywhere.

I stay in that moment.

I tell myself the truth.

And I am as accurate as possible. I gave birth to my son not knowing that I carried a dominant gene, which meant I had a 50 per cent chance of passing it to my kids and that we have a 90 per cent chance of developing tumours and cancer in a wide variety of places in our bodies.

When stuff like this happens, I feel guilty because my reactive, protective mom brain goes to beat me up and I think, *you gave this to him*, and it literally takes my breath away.

The TRUTH is I didn't "give" him anything. I catch myself and I say to myself, with kindness, "It was passed onto him and it's not your fault." I keep going back to that truth when my brain tells me that any of this is my responsibility.

I try to find one thing to be grateful for in that moment.

And usually I find way more than one. My big beloved son is such a rock, he takes things in stride, he is infinitely brave, always so beautifully kind (he thanks people when they give him his IVs) and he has a kick ass sense of humour even in the darkest of situations. AND we have an amazing doctor, who makes my son a priority and started his first treatment right away-she's amazing.

My son thought it was so funny that I was blabbing away to the doctor while she was looking in his eyes and commenting on how interesting it was that we don't get eye tumours at the SAME second she said, "There's one, and oh a couple others."

He said it was so hilarious how fast I stopped talking. It was funny. My jaw literally snapped shut. I think that sound could be heard for miles. That brought some levity and a wee joy spot to this crappy situation.

And the pièce de résistance is:

I don't fight it.

I do not fight my tumours or his. I don't like that we have them. I'm so disappointed and at times devastated, by my son's condition especially. But I cannot put on the boxing gloves and battle with this. I will always lose. I can't change this situation.

I surrender.

This circumstance "is" and I cannot do anything to change it, but I can give in and walk alongside this stuff, incorporate it into my life and take it along for the ride. The less I fight it the smaller it becomes. The more I focus on all the other fullness in life, the less I worry.

The not fighting, and rather letting it be, informs me of how I want to live and the more content I become.

I have had to learn the lessons.

We, OK I, worry and complain about things like my wrinkles and cellulite, but when bad things like this happen, I DO NOT CARE. I do not care if my income is less one month or my dishwasher breaks down. I do not even think about my wrinkles. I don't care. These things are minor and real-life stresses like losing your sight from a tumour put those little things in perspective VERY fast.

Whatever. Who even cares?

I take things in greater stride.

And finally, when things get hard, I make a mental list of what I can control and what I can't.

This HELPS ME SO MUCH! Do this people. It will save your life. I call it the parachute plan.

I have a saying that helps me let go of the gritty pieces on the "can't control" side, which usually sounds like "I'll have everything I need when I need it."

I don't always know what that looks like and bad things have definitely happened, but I have always made it through, and I continue to trust that this will continue.

Then I turn my attention to what I can control.

That list is usually longer than I think and simpler than one might imagine.

The "I can control" list usually starts with me being more present and really being with the people I love. When this happens, I become more spiritual, I joyfully exercise, and I become more intentional overall.

Surprisingly, I experience the most exquisite joy spots because life, even the hard parts, are so rich in meaning and gifts that I am most often in awe of the goodness I've been given.

This part of the journey to treat those tumours (it can take years) has just begun but I hold onto hope that we can navigate this with the grace, trust and wisdom that always accompanies us. I just need to remember that I will always have what I need, when I need it.

There's nothing that solves every problem and there are tragedies that hit us which are beyond devastating but using techniques that bolster our resilience can help soften some harsh experiences. It can make us better, not bitter, so more joy can sneak in.

Surprisingly, in the worst of circumstances there are the most exquisite joy spots because life, even the hard parts, is so rich in meaning and gifts. You don't want to miss out on them. They don't take away the grit, but they make the grit easier to take.

And trust! You will get through this, no matter what, we all will.

Reflections

Answer the questions from the gut, no editing, and keep writing until you feel "done."

Do this exercise frequently if you are experiencing tough circumstances.

1. First of all, feel the feels, all of them.

What are you feeling?

What do those emotions tell you? Do they bring up thoughts? Are they accurate?

Try to notice the emotions as if they are outside of you. Don't overthink them.

2. Tell someone how you feel.

Who are those people you trust? One or two people are plenty.

Reach out to them and tell them how you're struggling.

3. Stay in the moment.

Live where your feet are. Don't *future surf* and worry about what could happen.

4. Tell yourself the truth

What am I telling myself about the situation?

What's the accurate truth?

5. Try to find one thing to be grateful for.

There is ALWAYS something to be thankful for: being on time, having a car, being able to breathe-find something. What am I grateful for?

6. Don't fight it.

What am I fighting?

What am I willing to let go of?

7. Decide what you can control and let go of the rest.

Make a list of what you can control and how you will use that to your advantage. For the things you can't control, think of a saying, a statement that helps you in those "stuck times."

What can I control?

8. Learn.

There are always things to learn and integrate even in the hardest of times. This is where wisdom comes from. Lean in and learn.

What are you learning about yourself? Your life? Others?

Chapter 24 (P)

How Do I Hold Both?

I was drinking a glass of prosecco (heaven in a glass as far as I'm concerned) when my doctor called at 7 p.m., the evening following my abdominal ultrasound.

I had a pancreatic tumour that had disappeared six months prior, and my partner and I were celebrating because the tech had mentioned during the ultrasound that day that there was a mark on my pancreas at the place it used to reside. I LOVE that this freaking miracle is tattooed on my organ, so we were out celebrating that.

I missed the call because of my bubbly cup of bliss, but when I listened to my doctor's message, the bubbles lost their lustre.

"Leona," started the message, "you have a new tumour on your pancreas. Given your condition and the rapid rate of its growth, and not having been seen on last scan, it's concerning"

How do you go from joy to worry and stress?

How do you hold that?

In this case, I ordered a glass of red wine. Always thinking *what's next* and wine, chocolate or coffee rarely disappoint.

I had no more details so the next day I spent time trying to track down the results and get a hold of the doctor.

I always joke that I am not Type A, I'm more a middle child, B+ kinda gal, but when someone knows something about me that I don't, I get focused. I stopped short of creating a plan to break into the doctor's office to get my sticky fingers on my results. I had no luck in tracking down any more details AND managed not to commit a crime (super proud of myself).

The doctor finally called me back that evening and repeated what she had said the night before: concern based on growth rate (implying cancer, without speaking it), an MRI will be booked to look at it and hope that it's a benign "new kid on the block," (which can still cause issues but is not as worrisome), to add to the other eight tumours I have.

So how do you juggle joy of having a tumour disappear and the worry of the new tumour?

I didn't know exactly.

I did know that we are hardwired to focus more on the negative than the positive, but I didn't want those "wires," to hijack this experience. I wanted to balance both.

One does not wipe out the other.

I'm still trying all this out. My hope in writing about it is that it might help you explore things too and that we can be in this joyful muck of life together.

I'm continuing to be grateful for my missing tumour, everyone agrees that was a miracle. I don't know how many times that happens, but I know it's very rare. I'm not holding out for a miracle for the new one, but I continue to think about my miracle mark and feel gratitude.

I don't want to fear this tumour. I've been there, and although there's some fear in the initial shock, I know that it can fade and that it does (hallelujah-I hate the feeling of shock.)

I'm not grateful for this new tumour but I don't want to be at war with it either. People talk about "fighting" cancer. That's SO not my thing.

I've started by visualizing the "new" little guy everyday. I tell my kids I picture a baby tomato (like Bob in the kids show *Veggie Tales*) in a leather jacket (I have no idea why) except that my brain is mostly run by a fun five-year-old, and humour, especially tumour humour, helps everything.

My kids suggest not to make it such a rebel so perhaps I will make it more gentle-a Buddhist monk wearing orange robes-type a guy. Time will tell.

I have a morning ritual where I send people loving kindness. I pray for all sorts of people to "Be well, be happy, be peaceful and be loved."

I start with that as a prayer for me and I picture my "extra bits" that I host in my body and send them love, in a hope that they will behave and we can live long and prosper together.

I am asking my body what it needs to be healthy and happy and I do what it says-lots of veg, exercise, more naps, more holding hands with my beloved and being even more present with my loves (that includes my clients-I have the best job on the planet and love coaching soooo much).

I am also exploring ways to experience more joy.

Life is P R E C I O U S and meant to be lived. If I could shout that from a rooftop I would. I just might. ;)

If I'm more focused on finding my own pathway to joy and supporting others as they find theirs, I'm so much more in the flow of grace and gratitude and what's an extra tumour when your life is so full of goodness that you don't even think of the wee issues in your tissues?!

That's the goal anyways. This is my balancing act and most likely yours as well. Let's hang out on this teeter-totter of life together. I know we'll find the grace to move through it.

Whatever you are struggling with right now, would you consider sending that more love, more peace, more of whatever you feel it needs. Try it. Even within a week I noticed such a different feel around the thoughts of having a potentially cancerous pancreatic tumour.

Try to send your aches, those sore spots in your life, some loving kindness. See how it changes things.

Search for a loving kindness mediation in video form (just listen to it) or find an audio recording and listen to it. It will go something like thinking about yourself first and others after. You will repeat these types of phrases. May I be well. May I be happy. May I be peaceful. May I be loved. Then do the reflections below. Check out the meditation app called *Insight Timer*, it has options there for the loving kindness meditation that are so good. :)

Reflections

What did you notice during the meditation?

What was helpful?

What will you take away from the meditation?

Chapter 25 (M)

I Wish You Had a Tumour

Sorry, I kind of do.

If someone wishes that for you, you might want to consider opting out of the friendship.

I did actually think that, sorry (ish), please keep reading.

I was prepping for the MRI of my pancreas to check out the new tumour and I felt such deep joy. I felt so present and in tune with what mattered, it was weird, awesome, joyful, AND so unexpected.

Each moment took on a new sense of sacredness.

I was mindful of the fact that I wouldn't be able to eat or drink for six hours before the test, which was inconveniently at 2:30 p.m. I HATE that part of MRIs. Me being thirsty and hungry are not a good combo. Hangry Leona is not pleasant.

I wasn't resentful of having to starve to death (a small miracle, OK HUGE) but was reminded of the fact that every other day of my life I can eat and drink anytime I want-whenever I want. How fortunate I was to live this incredible life.

Life is precious and reminders of this preciousness of life have been even more evident in the last few weeks.

The other day, I heard a story about a woman who woke up next to her 48-year-old husband who had died next to her in his sleep. He had been perfectly healthy. My niece's boss was killed after being hit by a pipe in a robbery gone wrong. We have no guarantees and to be here, in this moment, is an incredible gift.

YOUR LIFE IS PRECIOUS.

I don't like saying life is short because some of us will live to be 100 and that's a massive bonus, but I do know that life is an amazing gift and we take so many ordinary moments for granted that could otherwise be savoured if only we reminded ourselves to slow down and take in the goodness that is found every day.

For me, my reminder is the new tumour and that's why I had the crazy thought, I wish *everyone could feel this*. Clearly not actually have a tumour and the potential loss of a pancreas, but feel the incredible, positive emotions that I was feeling. This tumour has become a gift in a sense.

While I would never wish you ill health, I would wish you a loving reminder that your life is a gift, that what lights you up is your gift to bring to the world, and to please shine some light on the goodness that only you can bring to us, in your own way.

Reflections

What are your favourite feelings to experience?

What will you do to feel more of those?

What will you do less of to feel more of your favourite feels?

What practices will you make part of your daily routine to feel more of what you want to feel?

Consider starting a gratitude practice or keeping track of how often in a day you felt your favourite feelings. Savour the goodness!

Chapter 26 (M)

Nothing Is Wasted

Life can change unexpectedly and what matters is how we roll with those changes.

Turns out that the pancreatic tumour I was diagnosed with and thought I had, did not actually exist. I found out six weeks later.

That tumour was something that the ultrasound picked up, but the MRI results came back and showed there was no new tumour. The ultrasound was apparently inaccurate, and the docs think that the growth was not there to begin with. I was initially grateful and then I was also pissed off.

I thought,

Why did I have to live like I had pancreatic cancer for six weeks?

What a freakin' waste of time.

I felt horrible for dragging so many people into my stress.

And then I thought,

Nothing's wasted.

That little non-existent "guy" reminded me of the incredible gift of life. It reminded me that life is so precious, and I don't want to waste a moment.

It reminded me to worry less and love more.

It reminded me that the darkness and the shadowy places in my life make the colourful moments that much more vivid.

It's hard to hold onto that but I needed to.

So, do you.

I first heard the phrase *nothing is ever wasted* the evening the pediatrician called to say my son had a brain tumour many years ago. I was devastated but I was also in the middle of cooking a turkey dinner and could not have a full-on melt-down in front of my kids. Clearly.

Within an hour of the call, I was supposed to be leading an infidelity support group, so I called to ask my co-leader to take over for the eve.

I told him I was so grateful that I could stay calm, so I didn't spook my kids despite my broken heart from the news I had just heard. That was one thing I learned from going through an affair years earlier; managing to keep things as calm as I could for my kids (which I didn't always manage to do as well as I would have liked).

Then, my co-leader said, "Nothing is ever wasted."

That has stuck with me ever since. Everything we experience has some wee nugget of goodness in it that helps us in other times.

I've learned so much, adjusted to things and worked hard to create a delicious life, more in line with how I want my life to be. The experience of my marriage eroding was far from a waste of time.

My hope is that whatever you've been through or are going through, you will see a sliver of a gift in it that can be used later. I hope you know that *nothing is ever wasted*. I hope you find a spot of joy in knowing that.

The last thing I want is to be is trite. I am not saying that something awful like a child dying or some incomprehensible tragedy becomes something you're grateful for. What I am suggesting is that there is something that you learned or gained from that experience that has been helpful for you going forward. It's about finding some sliver of meaning.

When my mom died, I never thought anything good would come out of that. I felt like I lost my only parent. I was devastated. I look back now, and I still wish it hadn't happened, but I do know I would not be nearly as empathic as I am for those that suffer had I not gone through that. There are some things you can't know until you've had firsthand experience. I now work with patients with her and my condition and I'm not sure I would be doing this had I not lost my mom to this disease. That's not wasted.

How do you create meaning when you look back at what you've been through? Is there a sliver of joy as you recognize the good that came out of something so hard?

Reflections

Reflect on a tough time.

Looking back, what did you take from that hardship to help you become more resilient, more empathic? More…. you fill in the blank.

Nothing is ever a waste. Something good, even if it's small, can come out of it.

What is that for you?

Chapter 27 (M)

Count Your Blessings

Let's cultivate some more joy with a pivot.

Want more joy? Focus on what you have, not on what you don't.

"You can't eat mangos? What about watermelon? Bread? Potatoes?" my kids asked with disdain.

I have a pretty disciplined lifestyle when it comes to eating. Very low sugar; natural or refined.

My kids asked me to list what I can't eat. Let's be clear, I CAN eat those things, I just don't, as I've been following an eating regiment for four years to help myself stay extra healthy. Cancer loves sugar and I am at high risk for developing pancreatic and kidney cancer. I'm not too thrilled about that so I do what I can.

I tell my kids that we can talk about all the things I can eat, do eat, and do love. To be honest I feel so good, I don't feel restricted and I feel so happy to have found what works well for me. I never even think of what I can't have because there are so many yums that I can have.

That's what I focus on.

We are hard-wired to look for the negative. It's a primary setting in our brains as it will keep us safe by being on the lookout for danger. Except if we focus too much on the negative, the set point in our brain becomes even more negatively focused and guess how much joy there is there?

Not much, you guessed it.

Especially when things aren't going great, we focus on what we don't have, what we can't have and what's not going right. It's natural and normal and we never want to candy coat pain.

A bazillion years ago you didn't want to be meandering in the forest, chasing butterflies, unaware of danger lurking nearby, paying no mind to the saber tooth tiger's breath on your neck. You'd quickly become a juicy dinner.

News flash. For the most part we are fairly safe. At least from life threatening dangers.

We don't have saber tooth tigers and t-rexs running down our front sidewalks these days. Awful things go on in the world, but if we want to thrive in life, we need to counteract the hardwiring of our brains and focus on the positives.

We need to somehow balance our fears and worries, with the goodness in our lives.

We need to refocus on what we can do, what we do have and even the wee glimmer of goodness we have available in any moment.

We can choose to focus on what we do have, can have, can do, and do love.

If we don't, we're at risk of living under a dark cloud and slipping down the slippery slope of seeing the dark side of things and life's problems as all pervasive.

One of the key factos in developing this kind of resilience is seeing reality as it is. That this reality is not pervasive, meaning that it's doesn't impact every aspect of our lives.

This is the stink bomb of negative thinking, you'll hear it coming out of your mouth, "My life sucks," or "Things will never change," or my least fave "FML."

If we're going to find any joy in this life, we need to be careful with the words we use and the thoughts we think and, frankly, the people we hang out with; they can all increase negativity.

We need to, after honouring those shadowy caverns of our lives, think of the *I can, I do, I have*, places.

Those may be hard to find at times, but without a little sunshine in the darkness, we all might as well pack it up.

Sometimes, it may be the smallest thing that we can do or do have that can shift things around such as feet that move, sun on our faces or strawberries in our mouths.

When the *don't haves* grab you, perhaps some time honouring the pain might be in order. Honouring them, by being mindful enough to recognize the thoughts and the feelings that come with them and then douse yourself with some self-compassion and then move to what you do have and what you can do.

And when you find yourself in that dark place of "life sucks," or "of course this happened to me," or "bad things always happen to me," try to change perspectives and notice the spaces that the light shines through for you. Even in the darkest places, there is always something good, always.

Let's focus on the things you can do…

Reflections

What do you say to yourself when something stressful happens?

What would be more helpful to think or say when things get challenging?

Think of something stressful? How could you consider this as an opportunity and area for growth?

How will you change how you talk to yourself about this situation to be more positively focused?

Chapter 28 (E)

Are You Living In The Red Zone?

I have seen at least half a dozen clients and friends, this week alone, who are living on the edge.

They are running full tilt; working, volunteering, managing households, cooking, coaching and they are moving full speed ahead.

I see this and it scares me.

Work needs them, their kids need them, teams need them…and it's taking its toll.

Is this what we're made for?

Running at a sprinting speed over a marathon distance?

I don't think so.

I'm not throwing stones from a glass house. Please hear me out. I have been there.

I didn't even know I was there until I got sick.

I am one of those people who very rarely gets sick. I haven't had a cold in seven years, although I have had the stomach flu and some back issues, lest we forget how dramatic those moments felt for me. ;)

The point where I hit the wall was when I was homeschooling my kids (I know, whole other book ;) and no worries they turned out great despite who their teacher was for years), working part-time, taking the kids to their activities, cooking a nice meal every night and responsible for all the household chores. If someone had told me to slow down, I wouldn't have known how to or why I would even consider it. I felt tired, but still very capable of managing it all well.

One day I woke up not feeling well and my heart was racing. Later that day, I was achy and wiped out. This bloomed into a fever that lasted over two weeks, and a heart condition that stuck around for 6 months. I lost 30 pounds and developed chronic pain that lasted for over half a year.

The doctor was doing all she could. I was tested for leukemia three times and every autoimmune disease around. I had to homeschool my kids from the floor some days.

Eventually, I ended up at a therapist's office with severe anxiety, thinking that I was never going to get better.

I had reached the end of my rope.

There was nothing left.

When I originally caught that bug, my body disintegrated. It couldn't keep going at the pace I was going. So, it flattened me.

I was nothing of what I once was, although even then I didn't take a break from cooking, cleaning, and teaching the kids. I just trudged through. Half dead.

I was wrung out. With the help of my therapist we settled on very small goals to focus on per day, so I felt less shame about how I was trudging through my life.

- smile at the kids one time each day,
- connect genuinely with the kids one time per day
- try not to worry about dying and be more present

OK, there was a fourth. I was told I had to stop making casseroles.

I had 23 casseroles in the freezer. I had developed OCD. Obsessive Casserole Disorder, so I would have food to feed my kids if things got worse or if the leukemia diagnosis came back positive. I wanted to be ready. I wanted my family to have homemade meals no matter what was happening to me. (I don't think I've frozen a casserole since-good therapy works people!)

I will never live at that pace again-ever. I began to even hate the word busy.

I am allergic to "too busy." I don't even use the *B* word and, if I do, I know it's time to reign things in.

When I see people going at an all-out pace, I want to shake them and then lovingly scoop them onto my lap and open their eyes to see what they're doing.

Your kids, partners, team, and workplace want you to be alive, not wrung out. They want you to say "no" so you can say "yes" to life.

We all need a buffer so if something happens, we have the resources to weather that storm.

Build a buffer. You deserve that.

I'm not saying we don't have seasons busier than others, but when that pace is relentless-there will eventually be a problem; either the disintegration of your health or your relationships, or your mental health…it's all too expensive.

What will it take for people to see that energy, immunity and health are limited and precious resources?

My heart breaks for the overextended who keep "doing" because they can or someone needs them or they feel alive when they help others or their kids will be disappointed if they don't get to participate in a couple of sports or, my fave, "if I don't do it, who will?"

Here's how to live a great life.

Scale back.

Don't offer help.

Skip a kid's game or practice.

Take a day off work.

Get takeout.

Be really brave and take a day off without pay if you need to.

Please listen to your body.

Give it rest.

Be accountable to someone else for not taking anything else on.

Assess what's on your plate and take off a few things. I don't care if you have a plate full of what you're good at and even what brings you joy. Try living at 80 per cent, OK, even 95 per cent capacity, so when life fills up a bit more you still have room and the resources to live life to the fullest.

Life is so precious and so are you. I want to skid across the finish line with you, happy and healthy (and diaper free-to be clear) at the ripe old crinkly age of 101, having experienced delicious spaciousness and grace that can only be found with the richness of free time and ease.

Ease up just a wee bit and see what goodness seeps in. I imagine you will also notice more joy.

Reflections

What's on your plate?

What are some glaring energy drains that you'd love to let go of?

What permission do you need to ward off the torrent of *shoulds*?

Permission to:

Permission to:

Where do you want to ease up?

What boundaries do you need to put in place in order to live more fully and less busy?

Chapter 29 (A)

Squirrels at a Rave

I do not have ducks and they are not in a row.

I have squirrels and they are at a rave.

I saw that saying on Facebook a couple of weeks ago and literally burst out laughing (LBOL).

That describes my brain and, sadly, my actions at times. I know I have a hard time sticking to one task. Maybe I'm normal, maybe I do actually have serious issues.

I'm mildly concerned that I've damaged my brain from having too many balls in the air for a wee bit too long or from my brothers sticking a large can over my head and hitting it with a hammer when I was four. As a last resort I can blame my brain tumours, which is a card I can pull, and nobody messes with it. :)

Anyways-see, even there I seem to have gotten distracted. SO many options and directions to be pulled in. I hate feeling scattered and I've even taught classes on productivity, but we all fall off the wagon, so lately I have been trying to observe where I get off track.

There are mornings where I've tried to brush my teeth and put on my jewellery at the same time or brushed my teeth and fold laundry. It was only when I slowed down did I notice that I was not actually brushing my teeth AT ALL.

I CANNOT BRUSH MY TEETH WITH NO HANDS.

At this point you're probably considering the brain tumour issues option listed above. I'm with you, believe me.

I will start putting on my makeup and decide to get dressed mid-way, only to tidy a few things in my closet, while I'm half-naked, and then go put on earrings, answer an email, do my hair, put on a bracelet, go to my office, pull my client files for the day, realize I have half my makeup on when I pass a mirror, put on water for tea, go back and complete makeup, go back to my office, have a client call and get my day going. Oh, right. I have to boil the water again. I forget about my tea.

WHAT IS WRONG WITH THIS PICTURE?!

I'm not going to beat myself up. I'm just observing after all (even though I do feel like a bit of a nut job). I am choosing to laugh at my behaviour and learn from it.

Your ducks may be so much more in a row than my raving, albeit cheerful, squirrels, but I think we could all learn to be more effective in our behaviour and processes.

This is what I'm doing to at least have my squirrels start a reasonably good conga line at their dance party:

1. I'm SLOOOOOOWing things down.

2. I've been gently observing myself.

3. I'm open to trying new things-experimenting with what fits for me. Like not leaving the bathroom until I am done there.

4. I'm intentional about building in new processes.

5. I complete small tasks before moving to the next one.

6. I get help if needed.

I work with a coach, who has a VERY good sense of humour and a gentle squirrel-loving demeanour and she has been helping me slow down and assess what I need more of and less of. I'm also hiring an assistant to brainstorm where else the squirrels are hiding nuts in my office and businesses.

I am happy to report that you will no longer find me half-dressed, with my makeup half done and files in my hands. I do have to remind myself not to do anything until my routine items are completed. These are perhaps small steps, but it feels great.

Although I am still forgetting about my boiled water, I'm blaming that on my age. ;)

Where are your squirrels raving?

Reflections

1. SLOOOOOOW things down.

2. Gently observe-your *rave* might be going full speed ahead-that's OK-no judgment. What's chaotic in your life right now?

3. Be open to trying new things-you may need to experiment with what fits for you. What would you be willing to try to do differently?

4. Be Intentional about building in new processes. What processes need to be put in place to make life less crazy?

5. Complete small tasks before moving to the next one. Make a list of your tasks. Prioritize and put in your calendar. Bunch like items like phone calls.

6. Get help if needed. Who will you ask for help with your specific needs?

Chapter 30 (M/E)

You Get to Decide

It's your choice how you live your life.

Joy is created or depleted by the decisions you make. You decide.

It sounds so simple but it's not always so easy.

Last week, I drove by a very popular café that was closing up at 4:30 p.m., as it does everyday, and thought, *why would they close so early? They could be packed until late into the evening.*

Yesterday, I dropped my car off at the mechanic and I briefly lamented that they didn't have a courtesy car to drive me home. Who does that?

I've worked with a coach who never did sessions in person, only over the phone-no matter what you offered in compensation; she did not budge.

What do those three businesses have in common? They run their businesses and, in turn, their lives. Not the other way around.

Business owner or not, you are the CEO of your life. You decide what you want things to look like.

As I've emphasised throughout these pages, time and energy are our most precious resources and we can live at times like we will always have enough of them.

I used to coach in the evenings and on the weekends. I loved those clients but when I looked at my calendar, I felt heavy. I thought I *had* to do those sessions because the clients requested them. I didn't have many options since it was the only time the clients were available.

Was I actually telling myself that I was out of options-that's just how it is? I guess so.

Slowly I realized that weekends and evenings weren't working for me and, sadly, I could not work with some of those clients-but I also became clear on what my business and life boundaries were.

I noticed more clarity and, of course, more joy. YES!!

I stopped checking email outside of business hours and designed my businesses and life the way I wanted.

Flexibility-that's the name of the game for me now. I have different hours, will go on a walk mid-day, do what I want when I want to and see how that goes.

If you audited your life, is there anything that you would change?

I've known people who ran from one activity to another with their kids every evening. I remember doing that with my children and it was exhausting. I wouldn't go back to that era of my life for all the money in the world.

"We were tired of running around and never seeing each other, so we took a year off," a friend told me a year ago.

YUMMO! And super courageous.

How do you decide what's not working for you? Some things are very obvious. Maybe you feel like you never get a break from work and you decide to not check email in the evenings.

Period.

There are a few ways to start with the subtler ones. Trust your gut, forever and always, to guide you in what's right for you.

Make a list of what you don't want to do. Don't get caught up in not doing them. You can work on that later or perhaps change things up around how they do get done.

If you look at your calendar and you have a negative physical response and feel resistance to something listed there-that's a sign. Maybe your chest feels heavy for a minute or your stomach clenches-take notice of that. I'm not saying you're not going to do it, but you may consider options of how to do it-more on that in a minute.

It's also worth doing an inventory of everything that's on your plate and dumping everything that you are currently managing. Add what's floating in your brain and dumping that out too. I call this a brain dump. (See tool below)

You may need to write yourself a permission slip, or seven, to help deal with some of the feelings of guilt or shame as you work through this. You can contact me anytime if you need some support.

If this *dumping* is your thing-go down that list of time consuming goodies and attack it.

Reflections

Dump, Defer, Delegate, Do (best stress relieving priority setting tool).

Write down everything that you have to do. Everything that comes up matters.

Categorize each item with one of the D's.

Dump. Defer. Delegate. Do.

Dump-get rid of-never to be seen again.

Defer, put it off to another time-put it in your calendar to consider at a later date but do not need to take up space in your brain right now.

Delegate (Love this one!) Ask for help, hire help, do what you need to in order to get this off your plate.

Do-get it done, put it on a list, prioritize the list and write down the very first step to take to completing this task.

Bunch like tasks together such as booking appointments and then book those chunks into your calendar.

You don't need to make radical changes; even a wee baby step in the right direction can be very helpful.

Here's the good news-you're not stuck-you can change things up. You can make a few small changes in your schedule, re-prioritize, ask for help (or hire someone). Remember, you're your CEO. Decide what would make your life simpler and a whole bit sweeter.

Chapter 31 (E)

Important Versus Urgent

Stephen Covey, a well-known author, uses this as an idea of prioritizing.

He suggests beginning with the end in mind and then plan backwards. This means plan with where you want to end up and move backwards from that target.

I often use this strategy in my business and with clients.

What's also been very helpful is looking at what's important versus urgent. (*Essentialism*, Greg McKeown). We desire to live based on what's important but so often we're dictated by the tugs of urgent.

It's about where you want to be at the end of your life. Once you determine what you want to create in specific areas of your life, you start to plan and implement a strategy.

This hit me like a ton of bricks. Even though it's simple and I know it in some ways, I don't always operate from this perspective and I soooo easily get off track.

This week, I've been noticing where I'm focusing on what's urgent instead of what's important. I notice how often I'm answering a text or email (urgent), instead of listening to my kiddos (important. Gulp!). I can be a brutal multitasker at times and that's not the worst of it. Lest we forget my raving squirrels?

I fill up my days with what feels *important* only to realize I have been strung along by what feels *urgent*.

I spent a day with my first coach, who had terminal cancer.

I took her to an out of town doctor's appointment. In order to get back in time for a meeting I had with a client, I would either have to rush or be late or arrive in a panic.

This dilemma made me think of the day my mom was dying and I was a maid of honour in my best friend's wedding. I went to the wedding and missed being by my mom's side as she died. The wedding and the obligation felt so important but in hindsight, I wish I had been with my mom and honoured what was really important to me.

With that in mind, I contacted my client and asked to move our appointment to the next day so I could savour time with my beloved coach rather than be in a rush. It was a small thing, but it brought me such deep joy to not have to be in a hurry, in which would most likely be the last time I got to spend with my beloved friend.

It was an incredible honour to spend time with her. In her words, she felt like she was straddling both sides; life here and what lies beyond. That perspective had given her great clarity about what really was important to her.

I wonder, if I were dying (and in truth we all are), would I be scrambling; chasing the urgent, trying to chow down on every last morsel of everything life had to offer? Or would I feel I had lived life in such a way that I had always been primarily focusing on what was truly important, and that the end of life would just prompt me to savour life more deeply?

My obit could read:

Mom spent time with us but texted, answered emails and cleaned while we talked. (and frankly some days it still might–I am so a work in progress)

That's not what I want.

At the end of my life I want to have focused on what's ultimately important to me and design my life around that.

I've audited how I spend my time, and I see where I am doing what appears urgent, skipping over important. Like skipping a walk or meditation and answering emails instead.

Focusing on what's important to you takes clarity and courage; setting boundaries, asking for help, readjusting to navigate towards what really matters.

Begin with the end in mind. What's really important to you?

Reflections

What do you want your life to look like?

What do you want your life to be filled with?

What's urgent that gets in the way?

Write your own eulogy. Yes, I mean it. It will change how you live when you see how you want to be remembered.

Set aside some time for those *urgent* things (there are ways to remove some of those "to do's" from your list)-I can even help with all of that, contact me. It's part of what I do as a coach to support people and help them to not lose sight of what's important.

Now reset your priorities and set your goals based on what's really *important*. Focus on what needs to happen in order to accomplish your primary focus.

Reread your eulogy often to set your priorities and create the life you really want.

Chapter 32 (R)

MRI or CAT Scan?

If you've ever had an MRI or a CT scan (often called a CAT scan) you know they each have their own drawbacks. If I had to choose one, I would pick the CT scan as it's fast and way less squishy compared to the MRI's I've had.

Don't panic, this chapter is not about comparing medical devices; keep reading.

An M.R.I. (not the big, claustrophobic medical device but rather the acronym) can be used to transform how we choose to look at the world.

M-MOST

R-RESPECTFUL

I-INTERPRETATION

I love this idea because psychologically, we are wired to think the best about ourselves and our motives and the worst of others (youch)-just the way we are hardwired. This hardwiring gets in the way of lots of goodness and of course, joy.

 Can't do much about that. Or can we?

You snap at one of your co-workers and you feel bad but think to yourself, *I'm so tired, I didn't mean to snap, but I can't tolerate much today.*

If a co-worker snaps at us we are more likely to think, *what an A#%$@, they have no right to speak like that. What a freakin' crappy response, what's their problem?!*

The M.R.I. approach involves compassionate thinking, a wee bit of what has been proven to increase our happiness. I'll take some of that, thank you very much!

When someone doesn't treat us well, we can choose to think about what their suffering might be. Perhaps they're tired or something awful has been happening in their life and that's why they're reacting as they are. This softens our own reactions and increases the chances for empathy and a proactive response from us.

The alternative is what I call the "CAT scan". You know it. You've probably been there, the claws come out and you react in kind with how you've been treated. It feels good for literally a second, but not long term. It's a flat-out joy kill.

However, with the M.R.I. strategy, when someone gives you the finger while you're driving, you don't give it back (sorry, integrity is hard, I know). You think about what might be going on for that person to get so angry about something so mundane as driving. You respond, not with flipping them the bird, but with a brief moment of compassion, or even a wave, or smile.

It's an opportunity to "kill" another with kindness (OK, I may be stretching this example a bit far, but I think you get the point ;)).

For the next week, think about people and their circumstances through the M.R.I. lens and see what happens.

How does this increase your positivity?

What happens to your stress levels when you greet challenging people with compassion? Do you feel some joy well up when you treat someone who is trying to treat you unkindly, with kindness?

Use the Most Respectful Interpretation approach to stop making assumptions about other's intentions and see if it doesn't lighten your load a bit too. We could all use a little less weight on our shoulders. In the end, wouldn't it be great if everyone gave us the same benefit of the doubt?

Reflections

Think of someone or something you judge frequently.

What changes when you use the Most Respectful Interpretation of that person or that situation?

How does the M.R.I. technique change who you become?

See a joy spot or two?

Chapter 33 (M/E)

Be Your Own Science Fair

As much as I hate math, I realize more and more that I do love science. I love truth and am delighted to find it wherever it may be. Truth is always a joy spot.

I am constantly experimenting with things like what time of the day I'm more creative, more energized, more intuitive, and more productive.

Which habits support me, and which don't?

My reasons for the experiments?

Without the awareness of what works and what doesn't, I have no idea how to run my life or my businesses or help my clients run theirs. When we aren't aware, we are run by our unconscious mind and that's not always the best. We end up fighting with ourselves and what comes naturally.

Here's what I know-there's no one size fits all approach and that's why I'm a coach primarily and then a consultant. Coaching helps people discover what works for them and consulting helps tells them what works across the board.

We all long for the simple answer. Thinking things like, *if I work out five days a week, I'll look a certain way.* Even better, *if I cut out "the starchy stuff," I will lose weight and never struggle with my size.*

Perfect, all sorted!

Our brains even reward us with a hit of dopamine, think a spark of joy, when we think we have found a pattern.

PLEEEAAASE! I so wish life were that simple.

Nothing works for everyone. I've gone to boot camp five days a week and have looked pretty much exactly the same as when I started three years prior.

I can't eat fruit, or I put on weight and have only sniffed simple carbs in years. Damn they smell GOOOODD!

I've told my son we cannot have Doritos in the house as I'm a card-carrying addict of those damn things. It's my gateway drug. That's me. That might not be you.

The more we know ourselves the more we can make sense of what works for us.

I took an online test recently to find out what my motivational tendency is and that helped reinforce who I am and what motivates me. (You can take it here: quiz.gretchenrubin.com.)

I am called an *up holder,* meaning I'm internally and externally motivated. Basically, give me a rule and I will follow it (except for speed limits-sorry). People with this type of motivation style get lots done but we can be very rigid (I reiterate VERY RIGID) but when the sun is shining bright and we are balanced, we're disciplined and not too "clenched" about it.

I can be pretty goofy, don't take myself too seriously and in some ways, am easy going. Nevertheless, I do not run my life in an easy going manner, and it feels even weird to see how rigid I can be.

I wake up early. Most days around 5 a.m. I never miss a workout (if I'm not injured) or my morning meditation time. I have coffee at set times. I go on dates on set days, you get the picture. It's not bad, the structure supports me, but I am a wee bit envious of people who are spontaneous.

I've been in business for almost 20 years. I remember starting off in my laundry room. I was at my desk, feeling myself slowly die, while looking at a 50+ page business plan that someone had developed for me.

OK – windowless laundry room, anyone can sort out that that is not a great work location. My inner sunshiny five-year-old needed windows and needed to be able to see outside.

A 50-page business plan to follow? Ya, no thanks. I can barely follow a one-page recipe never mind 50 pages of mind-blowing boringness (I recently found it and burned it).

Turns out, I did OK without it.

On top of all of this, I was cold calling potential clients.

Cold calling. The thought of it makes me die a little bit. My number one value is connection. Cold calling is virtually a value violation for me. It feels so disconnected.

All of the above made me feel like I was a nut job.

In the trifold display of the science fair project of my life called, "Leona runs a business," there can be no windowless office, huge daunting detailed plans, and inauthentic connection with people.

My improved business plan in my science fair project of my life has two to three over-arching strategic goals. These are ways to grow my business for the year and tactics around how I might do that. You don't need to run a business to do this either. This can apply to any work and home.

The way I build my business is by making authentic connections. Perhaps at events that are related to said business or chatting with people I already have a connection with. Or reaching out to people I know via email. SO easy!

When I started my first business, and I gave myself permission to set it up my way, I looked for connections I already had. I reached out genuinely, and things started to happen. That was how things have worked for me with my subsequent two businesses as well.

Lately I have tonnes on my plate and some of it terrifies me, like launching an online course, with videos, with ME on the video, talking, for doctors…and truth be told I've been paralyzed and I pulled back from lots of other things I *should* be doing.

This part of the science fair project is called "Leona has OAD" Obsessive Avoidance Disorder. For those of you who are unfamiliar with my particular form of pathology, it sucks!

Of course, this goes against my uber-disciplined side (upholder side) so while my gremlins beat me up for not accomplishing what I should be doing, I don't get much of anything done. Please tell me I'm not alone.

So, I've set aside the *shoulds*. As I mindlessly sit in front of my computer and let time pass, I think about conducting my own social experiments on myself. What will I do? Perhaps things I would never do. Things that seem like not a good idea to do (for me at least).

SO, I've been tapping into some badassery and doing random things to see if that changes things up.

Part of my disciplined side never allows for anything to be done around my home during the day, no laundry, groceries, etc. Either it's done before 8 a.m. or around dinner or it doesn't get touched. I have no idea how I became like this, perhaps fear of getting distracted and never getting back to work. Who knows?

The last few weeks of experimenting, I have been running errands, vacuuming, doing laundry, purging and even BAKING (I don't really bake, so this is really a surprise). In these wee science moments, I have noticed that the more I change up what I'm doing, the more I get done. Science fair success! Awesome, unclenching outcome!

Some might say that there should be more planning, a clearer road map and if that's your thing-Yay! Create the Google map for your life but know that the clearer you get on who you are and what works for you, the easier things become for you. That's a joy spot!

AND when you show up like that, authentic, intuitive, all mixed in with a wee bit of courage, the universe is waiting to reward you with a big smooch of joy and a boatload of ease.

That's what I love about us and our own science fair projects of what makes us, *us*. When people give themselves permission to run their lives and businesses based on their values and their uniqueness, things fall into place, feel more like play and there's even some fun to be had and in my case MUFFINS-yummo!

Conduct your own saucy science experiment!

Reflections

Where are you struggling with OAD-Obsessive Avoidance Disorder?

What are you avoiding?

What behaviours do you engage in when you are avoiding something?

What would you feel like if you started on that task?

Two options: Do something totally the opposite and see what happens.

Then do something to work towards what you're avoiding for five minutes each day and see what happens.

Chapter 34 (P)

Light as a Feather

As I write this, September is here and there's not enough pumpkin spice to soothe some of the angst that fall can bring.

Fall has such a different pace than summer. I hear people talking about it. Kids start back at school and activities, work picks up, vacation is mere pics posted on Facebook and a distant memory. (As I edit this, Covid is here and September is a storm of angst like we have never seen before-heaven help us all).

I was journaling about what I was worried about regarding fall and I wrote down that I was feeling concerned about the fullness of it. I'd abandoned the word *busy* several months ago, as you know. I despise the word and the feeling. For me, it means being dragged around by some craziness that I have little control over.

My life is full. Like a full plate. I put on it what I want. I do not consume or take part in what I don't want.

As September approached, I was fully aware of the increase in the bookings in my calendar. I began to feel the old feeling of me revving up to run a pace for the marathon that was ahead of me.

I became keenly aware that the pace may need to be more like a sprint over a marathon distance. My anxiety increased.

How am I going to do this?

Ugh, I can't wait for this to be…over.

That was my warning shot.

I can't wait for this to be OVER?

This? This being my life, OVER?

Essentially that's what I was saying.

I remember when my kids were little and I couldn't wait for them to sleep through the night, feed themselves and be able to bathe themselves. I don't think I was alone in that. It was tiring, but it was also filled with such exquisite beauty and I missed some of the joy of it because I couldn't wait to be "done."

Well, my last baby is moved out and moved on. I am done. I wish in some ways I could have slowed things down and not have been so eager to get to the next phase.

It's the same as feeling when a season, like summer, is coming to an end. I have lots of things going on and I don't want to wish it over. I love my life and I love what's being created, yet there's some anxiety that comes along with it.

There are lots of opportunities that are amazing, absolute blessings. Now that I'm not a young, tired momma, I do not want to feel like I'm sprinting from one opportunity to the next.

I do not want to "can't wait until I'm done this," with anything in this season.

In my journal (writing is therapy for me), I asked myself what I want the fall to feel like. I got the phrase *light as a feather* in return. I saw a feather gently moving with the flow of the air that carried it from place to place. Maybe that sounds woo woo, but the image makes me feel so much better than running too fast over a marathoner's distance, believe me.

I've asked myself these questions lately:

How am I feeling about what this season has in store for me?

Are there some places that I'm feeling resentment? Youch-this can come with terrifying answers.

I snapped at my partner the other day when he asked about an event that we're committed to. I am usually not a snapper and even I was surprised by my response.

That meant a check-in for me.

Resentments are always the first place to see where things need to be changed. It can take a ton of courage to change things, especially if you've been doing things the same way for a long time. It's so worth it though.

And finally, this wee *light as a feather* lands on the fact that, when I am in the moment finding joy and meaning where I am, I also lean into some trust that reminds me that I will have exactly what I need when I need it.

I may not have all the energy and resources I feel I need right now in the "bank," stored away so I can count it and stock pile it, but I will take good care of myself and I will have everything I need along the way.

AND so will you.

Look at your *always* list: working, making all the meals, cleaning the house, getting the groceries, planning all the things, planning date nights, paying the bills, working in a role that perhaps you don't love. Change things up and you'll create more space for some juicy joy.

Reflections

Please change things up by asking yourself:

What do I want to feel like as I move into this fuller place in my life?

What can I do to feel more aligned to my true self in this season?

What boundaries can I put in place to make sure I am more aligned with how I want this season to feel?

Is there any help I need to stay true to what I want when things are full?

Chapter 35 (M)

Why Is This So Hard?

I hate asking for help. HATE IT! I have been working on this for a long time and it's getting slightly better, but certainly isn't gone. You may notice that certain things you just keep working on. It's normal. :)

Asking for help has felt like peeling my skin off. I don't want to ask. I've tended to soldier through whatever it is I have on my plate and do it on my own. I am getting better, but still struggle.

Some days I can't. Sometimes I need help.

I've felt like a failure because I struggled with even asking my kids to empty the dishwasher.

What's wrong with me?

Asking for help is hugely vulnerable. First of all, there's that. We all want to be seen as independent and self-sufficient and needing help can feel like weakness. Sometimes it's also a way to avoid rejection or hurt when we ask for help and aren't met with the openness and cooperation we long for.

I went to a workshop on intuition and was going through the journaling prompts about creating the life of our dreams. I was trying answer the following question:

What stands in the way of living out your dreams?

The first thing I heard in my head was, *asking for help*.

I tried to put it aside and listen more deeply. The voice just seemed to get louder.

I hate these moments (and love them because intuition is our truth).

I like to blame it on my culture, being a kid of Dutch immigrants. We're fiercely independent and don't ask for help EVER. You can look it up. OK, not really, but any Dutch person will agree that we do independence well.

To the point that in my early 20s, I felt terrible for calling an ambulance for my very unconscious mother. I knew she'd be mad at us for calling for help. It took my sister and I close to 30 minutes to try and find another way to sort this situation out. We were considering putting her in the back seat of a car to avoid calling an ambulance. I told you this is serious-we don't ask for help. It's genetic.

What's up with that?! I was willing to put someone's life in danger to avoid asking someone for help. Yup!

We often don't ask for help to the detriment of ourselves and others.

Even paying for help can come with its own bit of shame. It can go against the unspoken rules.

Independence and getting help are not binary-they can work together, or so I've been told. Ahhhemmm. The struggle is real.

What have we made up about asking for help or allowing ourselves to feel like we need help in the first place?

What if asking for help is our way home? Our way back to the truth of what we need to live a fulfilling life.

What if the fullest life requires that you ask for help and allow others to help you?

What are those sticky areas that you feel too exposed to ask for help with?

Maybe it's:

Getting someone to clean your house.

Asking a co-worker for help with a project.

Asking someone to watch your kids so you can have a break.

Asking for volunteers so you have less on your plate.

Asking your partner to take on some household responsibilities.

Accepting money when things are tight.

What the heck?! Accepting money? Insert sound of needle scratching straight across a moving record-STOP THE BUS!!!

It seems that financial independence is held in even higher regard than anything else. There's a feeling of such shame to accept money in a tough time.

No way-not me! NEVER!!

But things happen. I'm talking about losing your job or getting ill and having the bills-the regular ones like food, heat, shelter, pile up. We rarely let someone know of our troubles, never mind allow them to cover a bill for us.

What if that's actually holding us back-holding us back from being loved by another or being cared for as part of a bigger community?

What if we're so deeply ensnared in the grip of fierce independence that we're not allowing ourselves to rest in the nurturing, provisional arms of another, whether that is another person or a community?

What if we are holding back some mysterious and delicious circle of life that we're made for, that brings us home, home to ourselves and home to a deeper sense of purpose, and helps us access the life of our dreams?

I have reached out for financial help. I had to do that to run a non-profit. That was a HUGE stretch for me.

Not wanting to miss out on anything because of fear and my desire to avoid vulnerability, when I was launching JoySocks I asked four people who I admire and respect, to help me to create a JoySock footed world. I had started this after my son's brain surgery where we give away fun, goofy, gift-wrapped socks, called JoySocks to people in charities, shelters, and hospitals. (www.joysocks.ca)

It wasn't comfortable asking for help, but in hindsight, sitting around my kitchen table with these volunteers was one of the best things I've ever done. People were thrilled to help, and I was relieved to have some support. Shockingly for me, people felt joy in being asked. Who knew that my need brought them joy? They found their joy spots by helping me. Wow.

If getting help is the way back to you and diving more deeply into your dreams, then what do you need help with?

Reflections

How different would your life look if you asked for help?

What keeps you from asking for help?

If you dared, where would you ask for more help?

Chapter 36 (M)

Know Who You Are

We have to know our values to know joy.

Values don't seem like part of the joy recipe. I know.

We talk about them, and the businesses we work for might have them wallpapered in the company foyer. Who doesn't want to work for a business that says it values trust, integrity, and truth?

Only to find out that at the watercooler, people are talking behind other people's backs and at a team meeting you are required to use very specific language to ensure that some details are overlooked. This is when you quickly find out that truth and integrity are not actual values. We quickly feel disillusioned and even unsafe.

Turns out these values are crap, just wallpaper: nice to look at but nothing else.

Here's the truth.

Our values are who we are at our essence. They are who we are at our best (not perfect) and they light the way in dark times when we make hard decisions and when we want a deeper sense of fulfillment (aka more joy).

Values are our joy spots. Our anchors to our truth.

When they're not honoured, we feel emotionally triggered, usually by anger. For most of us, we aren't aware of our values and, even more importantly, what behaviours reinforce our values.

"A value is a way of being or believing that you hold most important," says Brené Brown.

Her research explains that values light your way as you move through life. She uses the image of a lantern to describe what values can be like in your life.

"There are no guarantees in the arena," says Brené. "We will struggle. We will even fail. There will be darkness. But if we are clear about the values that guide us in our efforts to show up and be seen, we will always be able to find the light. We will know what it means to live brave." Brené Brown, *Rising Strong*

I have 10 values, and I have boiled them down to two to rely on when things are extra tough. They are love and courage. These are the two most important values that guide me when things feel gritty and hard. Love includes kindness and respect and I use it towards myself and others. Courage helps me do what I feel is right and stay within integrity even when things are hard. Courage reminds me to do brave things even if I feel afraid.

Recently I had a colleague launch an inaccurate complaint about me to an organization that I was providing services for. I was so shocked that she would do this. I wasn't so worried about the complaint because integrity is a huge value for me. It means you do what's right. So, I was trusting that would come out as the complaint was investigated. The incident was easily cleared up as I had done nothing wrong.

My natural reaction would be to feel angry (which is natural and normal) AND along with this, I would perhaps want to lash out at her. Most often this retaliation takes place just in my head. This time I chose to send her love every time I thought of her, that's it. It takes courage to do what's right. Lashing out is cheap and easy. Living into our values is good and right. I want that.

I know that only hurt people, hurt people. She must be very hurt to want to hurt me. I felt a spark of joy after all of this because acting with integrity and living out our values, even when it's hard, does just that. It brings us unexpected joy to live out of our truth.

If we want greater resilience, clarity, traction, and joy in life, we need to know our values. Values are what really matters to us AND how we define them and what behaviours reinforce them.

There are a number of ways to do this. You can go through a huge list and pick the ones that pop out at you, but we often end up with a HUGE list and not a lot of traction.

Which values light up your life in the darkness?

Here's a tool I use with all my clients. Give it a try.

Values Exploration/Reflections

Values are who we are at our core and when we are honouring them, our life feels fulfilled and rich.

How do we know what our values are?

Here are a couple of fun ways to dig them up. :)

Plan an imaginary dinner party and invite five to six people you admire. They can be people you have met or people who are well-known (alive or not).

Is there a certain place that you would hold the party? Would you dine in or out? Would you have music? This can help you see if beauty or creativity are values for you, or maybe it's something else.

Guest:

Guest:

Guest:

Guest:

Guest:

Look at your guests one by one.

Answer this question about each guest:

What is it that you admire about them?

What characteristics do they have that you would like more of in your life?

When you have your list of characteristics of each guest written down, look for any similarities.

Can you group those characteristics?

Perhaps you have words like-Respect, Honour, Integrity. Would all three of these words be values that stand alone? Or could one be a core value, and the others a list of supporting values and behaviours, serving to define the core value?

Your list might look like:

Value: Respect-
- honour

- good boundaries
- being present with people

Perhaps Integrity is its own value with components that fit underneath it.

Another good way to mine for values is thinking of what behaviours really bother you: late people, unkind people, stingy people, or my fave, inefficient people?

Behaviours that make you feel angry/betrayed/very frustrated:

1.

2.

3.

4.

When our values are violated, we tend to have a visceral reaction to it. If someone is late, what value is not being honoured? Is it respect, kindness?

You'll know when you find it. It will feel like a puzzle piece finding its way to the spot that it's meant to fit in.

Our values are meant to be honoured in a balanced way. Too much generosity could mean that we give all our resources and energy to others. We want to identify what the balanced value looks like in our lives and honour it with ourselves as well as others.

Write your values here, how you define them and what behaviours re-inforce them.

1.

2.

3.

4.

5.

6.

7.

How this worked for me. ;)

I admire Corrie Ten Boom. She was a Dutch woman who, during the Second World War, hid Jews and was dangerously involved in the Dutch underground. Corrie was ridiculously courageous and such a bad ass. She was a non-conformist and extremely resourceful, using whatever she had to do whatever she needed to do. The family ended up in a concentration camp as punishment for what they had done and even there she was kind and generous to others. She suffered and lost so much. Corrie lost her sister and dad in the camp, but years later, spoke of forgiveness and forgave one of her jailers when he approached her at one of her speaking engagements. I just love her.

I want to be courageous, loving, and generous when things are hard. I share those values with her.

My other guests are different, but they share similar things that I admire such as courage, kindness, generosity, and resourcefulness. These reflect some of my values too.

We feel the most fulfilled, and so will you, when we live by them.

How did we not get taught this in school??

When we are in situations that don't honour our values, we will often feel angry or frustrated. These are value violations.

Looking at value violations, one of the things that I despise in people is lack of transparency. It makes my head pop off. Transparency, which I define as courageous honesty, is an important value for me.

It takes courage to tell someone the second they have broccoli in their teeth and to not wait until I ask, two hours later, "Has that piece of broccoli been there the whole time?"

So, transparency goes on my values list. I know what it means and the behaviours it reinforces. People who know me realize that they must be transparent. No half-truths, no withholding of information. Here's the important part. I have to be courageously honest with others too. It's not just how I want to be treated; I feel outside of integrity when I am not transparent. It's a both/and situation. I will start to feel flat, unfulfilled, and unhappy if I am not living by my values. There's no space for joy when we live like that.

Most people have between five and 10 core values. We feel most fulfilled when they're all in balance. Even if you recognize two that light the way for you in dark times, you'll be way ahead of the game. For me, as I've mentioned, those would be love and courage. I could throw many of my values in the love bowl and courage encourages me to forge ahead even when I'm scared.

Reflections

Do the above values exercise. Boil them down to two that really guide you when things are hard.

Dive into your values. Know your values, know yourself. AND know more joy!

Chapter 37 (M)

Are You Done With That?

Then take care of it and move on.

Simple?

Not always.

There is little that gives me more joy than completing a task. Most days I have a long list of tasks and I love scratching things off the list. There is joy in completion. It's a joy spot.

I know people who write down what they've done after they're finished, just so they can see their list scratched off. It feels that good! Feeling some joy just thinking about this aren't you?

Productivity experts say if you have a task, like a short email that can be answered in less than two minutes, do so. If you have a couple of pieces of clothing lying on the floor, pick them up and deal with them before you go to bed. Those little completions go a long way and give us an overall feeling of well-being and increase our locus of control (fancy psychology term for feeling in control). Completing things gives us a wee smack of joy. Yum.

What about those bigger pieces in our lives and businesses that aren't complete?

Last year's taxes that we haven't done yet? Maybe we just need a couple more receipts.

A file that we have been meaning to address and haven't gotten around to in months?

A tough situation with a client who we have been putting off contacting because of overdue invoices? (I HATE this one).

The above examples can be energy drains and a drag on your brain's operating system.

If nothing else, take a wee step towards completion on a daily basis. Look around you. Put the cup in the dishwasher instead of in the sink, put away the empty laundry basket instead of leaving it by the stairs, tidy up your desk before you call it quits for the day, close off open tabs on your computer. You'll notice a difference.

When you're ready, you can take a look at the bigger pieces of your life and your business or whatever you do professionally that could use some completions too. Baby steps, but know, my friends, that on the other side is more room for possibilities, freedom and of course, joy.

A while back, I found a file that contained stale cheques that were a decade old. VERY STALE. I'd found them in the back of my filing cabinet. I held onto the file for a bit after I found it because I didn't know how to address the situation. Frankly, I was mortified that I'd lost them and now found them.

You see, I'd managed community memberships 10 years ago. I had put an envelope of six cheques to be cashed in a file. Then, I forgot all about it.

Until I stumbled upon them. Crap.

I physically felt heavy every time I saw them.

Even worse was the shame I felt. I currently run two businesses and a non-profit (that are managed happily by bookkeepers and accountants-thank goodness). All I could think was, *what would the president of the community association think of me if I handed her these 10-year-old cheques?*

It didn't matter. I had to complete this situation. I reached out to her and when I saw her, I told her my mistake and included a personal cheque to cover the outdated ones. I felt a weight lift as that situation was complete and I'd honoured my value of integrity. I owned my part as best I could and moved on. A previous shame-filled spot was now filled with joy. I acted inline with my values and I completed something I was dreading. Yum!

That was relatively easy to do compared to a relational issue that feels incomplete. Maybe there's a conversation that you have been avoiding because it feels hard or vulnerable. Or maybe it feels off for another reason.

It's hard to move on after people have hurt us or continue to do so, or after a relationship has changed or ended. What do we do with those incompletions?

Often, we feel like we need to do something and we don't even know where to start. Those places can be filled with pain. How do we move through it?

I often pass on a tool, a "simple" set of questions, for my clients to use to process what's going on.

I use this tool with myself to see where I feel stuck and to help me process what I need to do to move on. Sometimes the process can be a matter of journaling the answers. Sometimes it can take years; going back and working through the questions or even just using one that feels sticky and working through that one over a period of time.

The questions helped me when I was considering meeting my ex-husband's affair partner to speak of forgiveness and to close up that portion of my life. I knew I was OK and ready to move past that exquisitely painful time when, after going through the questions, I felt no emotional triggers or hard feelings.

This tool has helped me so much.

If you spend time with each question and sail through them with no reaction-you're probably feeling quite complete in that area and there's nothing more to process.

The questions are simple, but your answers may not be. The more intentional you are about the questions (like writing out the answers and burning them), the more you'll get out of them.

A friend wrote some of her answers on eggs and threw them at a tree. I love that completion process. (Sorry eggs and tree.) You decide what would feel the most meaningful.

Be sure to make a list of the emotionally tough places in your life that you feel are incomplete and then go through the following questions:

What am I willing to let go of?
What am I willing to give up?
What am I willing to take responsibility for?
What am I willing to forgive another for?
What am I willing to forgive myself for?

Take each of the areas identified as incomplete and determine which steps would help to facilitate closure.

When we have a feeling of incompletion, we so often feel that if we could just talk to the other person and work through a *completion* it would be so much easier. That's not always possible, and even the best-laid plans to have conversations in order to facilitate completion can still leave feelings of pain and incompletion.

The truth is that completion is about us. It starts and ends with us doing what we can and being intentional about creating our own completion.

You know you want to let some stuff go, here's your chance: Think of an area where you feel stuck, bitter, or think about a lot and can't seem to move on. Try these questions out.

Reflections

What am I willing to let go of?

What am I willing to give up?

What am I willing to take responsibility for?

What am I willing to forgive another for?

What am I willing to forgive myself for?

Chapter 38 (R)

Feels Like Fresh Baked Cookies for the Soul

When someone shows us genuine empathy it feels so good. To me it feels like a fresh-baked cookie, melting on my tongue. So dang good. You could use some empathy as you move through those last completion questions, too, I'm sure.

Empathy shows a deep understanding of another and drives away shame. Empathy drives connection. Almost like fresh baked cookies do. They both feel so good! Like melted chocolate goodness.

We are hardwired for connection. Belonging and a feeling of authentic connection are what fills us up. They are some key aspects of resilience and even increase life expectancy.

Dr. John Gottman, a relationship researcher, says that for us to be able to give feedback and have the other person be open to receive the feedback we must first communicate understanding (or something positive). Empathy is just that. It shows we understand and that we are with someone in their struggle.

It's a skill that can be learned and has very clear components, like a recipe! Yay for the empathy recipe! (Sorry, no cookie recipe included).

Think of the last time you were struggling, you shared it with someone, and they listened, didn't offer advice and were just with you. They're most likely an empathic guru. Keep that friend.

This comes naturally to some and can be a learned skill for those of us who are more remedial in the empathy class.

When I got diagnosed with my brain tumours many people told me how good it was that the tumours weren't cancerous. Of course, I felt grateful for that, but to get diagnosed with four brain tumours in one day is super stressful and my mom had also died from them. They may have been benign, but they still sucked.

I met a friend and she said, "I'm so sorry about your tumours, you must be devastated!" I felt so seen. It gave me space to talk about how scared I was. That was empathy.

When someone is suffering, we do not bring up the flipside or bright side of the situation. This drives disconnection.

You don't need an alternative perspective when you're struggling; that feels like a slap in the face. It will quickly become evident that you don't want to share your feelings with that person, as they don't seem to see you; they're seeing everything else but you, and that stings.

Another way deep disconnection shows up is with the words *at least*.

I'll write this again.

At least.

At least is a HUGE disconnector.

When my son had brain surgery, he had to walk with a cane for the first while. I mentioned this to a friend, and she said, "At least he's not in a wheelchair, you have so much to be grateful for."

I knew I had a lot to be grateful for, believe me, but it felt like a smack in the face when she said that. I was watching my formerly healthy child walk with a cane. I felt terrible for his struggle and I did not need to be reminded of other possibilities.

I needed her to see me and my struggle. Empathy does just that.

Here's how we bake up Empathy (chocolate chips optional).

Empathy recipe (Teresa Wiseman)

1.	We need to take on the other's perspective.

What empathy requires is that we set aside our judgments, our assessments, our interpretations and, as Teresa Wiseman, a nursing scholar who studied empathy, said, "We look through the eyes of another." Or, as we often say, *we need to step into the shoes of another*.

2.	Stay out of judgment.

Especially with kids and spouses. We frequently dive in and offer advice and try to fix the problem. Usually we do this trying to relieve pain but it's not helpful, not before we show understanding.

We must set aside our judgments. Even if you never would have done what this person has done, telling them that is not helpful and drives shame (the fear of disconnection).

My son called me after he crashed on his skateboard, going down a huge hill WITHOUT a helmet. He was very scraped up. I am a safety girl and normally, I would be super pissed off at him. I always tell him to wear a helmet. In fact, I have on many occasions mentioned that I will not change his diapers if he gets a serious head injury from not wearing one. (I know, I won't be winning mom of the year award anytime soon ;)).

By some miracle, I went to pick him up and said nothing about helmets. I kept my mouth shut and showed him lots of empathy. He was hurt and I chose empathy over telling him he should know better. If I felt that was important later, I could swing back and ask if I could talk to him about what happened and how I felt about it and give him feedback. (Update, he wears a helmet on that hill now, natural consequences have a way of changing people. :)

3.   We try to identify the emotion the other's feeling and communicate it.

We often don't know what to say when someone is struggling. The good news is one of the skills that came out of Wiseman's research is to simply guess what the other person might be feeling. In a situation of my friend seeing her ex with another person, I would feel hurt and angry at first. Express the emotions that you think they might be feeling.

I would say something like, "That must be so hard, I would be so hurt if I saw that." They might say, "I feel crushed." in return and then all I have to do is remember when I've felt crushed.

It doesn't need to be for the same reason. Our role is to name the emotion we think they might be feeling and then relate to the feeling that they express in return.

You might not feel that feeling at all about that situation, that's fine. We stay out of judgment regarding the situation and the feelings surrounding it. That's how we show up and really connect with someone who is struggling.

You're looking at it through their eyes, like you're crawling into their skin. My friend said she felt devastated and so I got in touch with that emotion in myself and felt that with her.

Some of you might be saying, "I'm too empathic, I'm a flat out, full fledged empath, I feel all the feels, I have no empathic immunity, if someone's feeling something, I'm feeling it too."

Just like looking through another's eyes, we do not take on the other's emotions. I am not saying that you might not feel awful with someone; that's normal, and if you're sensitive, that may be more intense.

4.   We take a mindful approach to the emotions.

We need to be mindful about our emotions and the emotions of others. In order to effectively show empathy to others, one must become aware of the other's emotions but not take them on. When my son crashed, I was scared and so was he. He was initially having some trouble breathing. So, I was mindful of the fear, but did not let it take over as I decided what the next steps were to care for him. Not easy, but very important.

Mindfulness, while being empathic, is a game-changer.

Someone might be very anxious about something that's coming up and when we talk to them, we start to feel anxious too. Anxiety is a highly contagious emotional affect but beyond that, it's a simply a feeling.

We need to hold it outside of us, recognize the feeling but not over-identify with it.

Don't take on someone else's feelings. You may feel anxious alongside the person you're supporting. Your brain might interpret the feeling and start feeding you doomsday messages saying, "Crap this is bad, avoid this, don't do this."

Instead be mindful, which sounds more like an internal dialogue, "This is anxiety, this feels scary, I'm OK right now, I'm doing my best even with these hard feelings."

Empathy, when done well, can effectively hold space for those that suffer, in the most effective of ways. It drives connection, heals an abundance of pain, and makes the space in your relationships a soft place to fall. We all need more of that.

Think of a recent experience where someone shared how they were struggling. Use the following framework to write down how you would have responded using the five components of empathy.

Reflections

1.   Take on the other person's perspective.

2.   Stay out of judgment.

3.   Identify the emotion the other's feeling.

4.   Express the emotions that you think they might be feeling.

5.   Take a mindful approach to the emotions.

Chapter 39 (R)

The Toughest Thing of All

Maybe not the toughest, but pretty close.

Clients and friends bring it up all the time.

What is this thing?

How to communicate what you need.

Most of us are very capable of exploding after we've held in seething resentment over not getting what we need. This is what we want to avoid.

We know how to show understanding, which is delicious. Empathy is so good. Now we need the courage to communicate what we need and want so we can decrease the chance of conflict. This is hard. I know.

One thing that I hear over and over from my clients is, "How do I give feedback, or ask for what I want?" Crickets. Rarely do we know how to do this. If we do communicate what matters to us it's often after we have shoved it down for months and it comes out in a rage-filled tirade, along with the always and never words.

There is little joy if you don't know how to communicate effectively.

Let's say someone is not coming through on something important. Maybe it's a project or emptying the dishwasher. Just like the empathy 'recipe,' this is a framework that you fill in with your details. This is about lowering defenses, so you need to spend some time prepping so you're not fuming when you start this conversation. Go back to the completion questions, if needed, from the chapter a while back to prep, if you're feeling charged up about this. It will help.

Here it is:

When this happened…

The impact or how I felt was…

The story or assumption that I made up was…

What I need is…

It's that easy!! Yes, well that part is, now you need to fill in the blanks and have the courage to speak to the other person AND try to avoid using the word you if the person tends to get defensive.

That framework looks like this, perhaps when you are talking to a member of your team who has not delivered their portion of the project work on time.

When this happened: "When the project got delayed after the time-lines weren't met, that set the whole team back." (You know that this was one person's fault, but you are trying not to use the word "you," unless you have to.)

The impact or how I felt was: "This felt really frustrating and disappointing for the team who had worked so hard meet the deadlines and delayed all deliverables now, so the client is not happy."

The story or assumption that I made up was: "The assumption that I made was that maybe you were in over your head or didn't ask for the help you needed in order to produce your part of the project on time."

What I need is: "What I need going forward or next time is for you to let me know if you're swamped or if you need help. We can support you and understand if a portion of his project will be delayed so we can all work together to meet the deadlines."

Then the other person can address what they were just told. This framework saves lives. OK maybe not that dramatic, but it absolutely saves relationships from resentment and erosion.

Another great communication tool is the communication sandwich. I was taught it as the crap sandwich as you put the hard to say *crap* in the middle of the sandwich.

Our brains love empathy and positivity, so start with something sincerely positive and empathic to start. I say sincerely because if it's not true or authentic, it will not prime their brain to receive the feedback and you'll be outside of your values. There is no joy there.

Then put in the part that's challenging to say. Perhaps it's feedback or a boundary.

Finish off with something encouraging or positive. Genuinely so.

Using the example above, the sandwich could look like:

"I know you've been working really hard (positive), or I imagine you must feel overwhelmed with all that you have on your plate right now (empathic)."

"I need you to let me know earlier if you can't meet the deadline. This set the whole project back."

"You're one of the most talented members of the team. I know we've learned a lot and we'll do much better next time."

For me I get a lot of invites to social engagements. I have to put up a boundary so I don't become overwhelmed. I do not do lunch or coffee with people. It is not my thing, so I want to kindly communicate that without needing to get into details.

To set a boundary, the sandwich script looks something like this:

"Thanks for reaching out, or it's nice to hear from you. I'm unavailable to meet you to grab a bite to eat. I'm free for a walk sometime if you'd like."

If that's not something I would like to do with that person, I say:

"I'm at capacity right now-hope you're doing well, wishing you all the best!"

Youch, that may seem a bit harsh, but it's authentic and true. That matters and if we want to create room for joy to stick around, we need to be genuine, as well as know how to communicate effectively.

Boundaries and feedback can feel challenging and bring on feelings of shame. Most likely saying to you something like, "Who do you think you are to say or ask for such a thing?". Shame always shows up when we are doing something courageous. It's how courage and being vulnerable work. Shame shows up.

Soften the shame you feel by giving yourself permission.

I give myself permission to tell the truth.

Permission to speak up about what matters to me.

Permission to be transparent about the truth.

Write it out so it can sink in.

Be sincere and be kind about what you need. That makes the world go 'round' and after you handle what would have otherwise been a tough conversation in a well thought out and gracious way, you will feel some goodness and joy knowing you did the best you could. That matters.

Reflections

What part of giving feedback makes you most anxious?

Where would you like to set a boundary?

What do you worry about when you have to set a boundary?

What could you give yourself permission for that would make this process feel easier?

What technique do you want to employ right now in a situation that requires some clear communication that you may be avoiding?

Chapter 40 (R)

Listen to Me!!!

"They don't listen to me!"

I hear it all the time from all my people.

More often than not we don't "hear" because we are too busy listening and deciding how we will respond in a conversation.

Often our responses can be in defence of something we did that's being brought to our attention.

Or we are genuinely trying to help so we are coming up with some brilliant solutions to solve the other person's problems. I prefer this one. :)

Or we don't really understand what's going on.

None of the above options work well.

It's not that we're coming from a bad place. So often we want to help ease pain. But when one shares a struggle with you, that's not what they're looking for-they want to be understood-that's it.

After attending a couples' retreat with Dr. John Gottman, the world's leading researcher on what makes relationships thrive, I learned some incredible tools that should be taught in every grade and level of post-secondary institutions. They're effective and easy to use. Plus, they change your life, so there's that too.

Gottman's work is so precise that, after watching couples interact for 15 minutes, he can predict with 91 per cent accuracy whether a couple will be together after five years. He and his wife, Julie, have developed specific ways to help people feel understood and listened to.

The truth is most arguments escalate when one of the partners feels unseen and misunderstood. We don't actually have to agree to have a deep and caring relationship. This applies to relationships at work too.

Think of when someone shares a struggle with you, and you go into problem-solving mode. Even those situations can end up in an argument and, at times, have you stumped as to how that even evolved to that point.

We've touched on expressing understanding and creating a deeper sense of helping others feel seen and understood in the previous chapters. Here's more from Gottman; he's the expert.

Step 1: Prepare yourself
- Shift your focus away from yourself.
- Postpone your agenda.
- Tune into the other's pain, even if you don't agree-empathy is magic.
- Try to see the situation from their perspective.

Step 2: Attune
- Ask open-ended questions that can't be answered with yes or no such as, "How does that feel?" "What's that like for you?"
- Do not ask "why?"
- Be empathic, which means trying to hear the underlying emotion and thinking of when you've experienced a similar emotion (not in the same circumstance necessarily). Tap into what that was like.
- Communicate understanding, "I can see why you feel like that."
- You are observing, not judging their experience or emotions.

A conversation might start like this:

Partner: "I'm exhausted with all the demands of the kids. Their school and activities are killing me. I can't carry on like this."

Your optional response: "You take on so much, I don't know why you get so worked up, ask another parent for help with driving a couple of times a week."

The conversation is wrapped up, quick and simple AND you're a freakin' genius! You solved yet another problem and even recognized one of your partner's primary issues at the same time! (Don't try this.)

If you're really brave, try out, "I told you not to sign them up for so many things, what do you expect?" Get ready to duck if you're going to lob that response. I'm joking-DO NOT TRY THIS.

Your partner is smart-they would have most likely mentioned that they couldn't figure something out and would like your opinion if that was the issue.

Another situation: Your teenager comes home and says she's getting teased at school. One could respond with some suggestions for finding new friends. Simple really! Dang we are good at this! Bring on the problem and we'll solve it!

But are we really listening? Do we really understand? Do we really see?

Wonder why some arguments escalate? Gottman says it is primarily from people feeling like they are not seen. They don't feel understood.

People can figure out their own problems. If they want your expertise, they will ask for exactly that.

In the meantime, try listening to understand, to see what's really going on. Perhaps there is more under the surface, and taking the time to really hear will create a new level of intimacy and a *deep seeing* of the other. This brings life and deep connection.

So, if your partner says, "I'm exhausted with all the kid activities. I can't carry on like this."

Try, "That sounds tough (guessing at what they might be feeling-you don't have to be right-empathy!), tell me what's going on."

Ahhh a blessed invitation to go deeper and explore.

They continue… you respond, "That is stressful…what else is going on?"

They continue or not and you say something like, "Is there anything that I can do?" or "Thank you for telling me, that means a lot to me."

By thanking them for telling you, they feel like you're in their corner, you are honoured to know what's going on for them. It takes courage to admit you're not a parenting superhero.

Sometimes arguments are fueled by the statement, "You never help me!" (Youch-that can sting!) Try the same technique that you used above and see how it works.

In the meantime, if you can:
- Overlook the attack (if there is one)
- Ask what's going on
- Guess/imagine what they might be feeling (empathy-damn you're a pro)

- Think about a time that you felt a similar way (may have been for a totally different reason)
- Listen to their world and get their perspective
- Set your opinion and perspective aside

So many arguments would be diffused, and intimacy would be greatly increased by you modelling this. You may also get more connection in return.

More love, more connection, more synchronicity.

More Yum-that makes the world spin on its axis a wee bit easier and you played a part in that. AND joy for doing something that's super hard, but so worth it. Thank you!!

Whether you are a leader, a parent, a co-worker, or a lover-this skill will make you a relational superhero.

Give it a try. Listen to understand and see what happens.

Increase your communication game! There are major amounts of joy in understanding!

Reflections

How do you feel about conflict?

What triggers, or makes it hard for you, during conflict?

What support do you need to help you during conflict? That might look like you letting the person you're talking to how hard this is, or maybe that you might ask for a break at some point (always make sure you set up a time to resume the conversation).

Use the above framework to have a better outcome when you are in a tough conversation. There is joy in understanding- A LOT!

Chapter 41 (P)

Just Get Over It

I'm sure you've been struggling at some point in your life and someone, perhaps with the best of intentions, said, "You need to just move on."

Perhaps they said, "Just forget about it."

Whatever it was, I'm sure they meant well and were hoping that by your suffering ending, their suffering might also be alleviated. It's a normal reaction.

It may be normal, but it's not right.

You don't have to get over it, not now, not ever.

I'd ask that you don't forget whatever it is that's tearing at your heartstrings.

It takes flat out courage to be with what makes us ache, with what keeps us awake at night and with what makes us start our day with a bag of ice on our puffy skin around our eyes. (Go with slices of cucumbers-easier on your skin, and a big hug to you if you're here xoxo.)

People who work hard to just get over it, forget about it, move on, risk dreadful consequences. They can become bitter, resentful, untrusting, and unable to experience true happiness. No joy, sorry.

Only three weeks after discovering my then husband's affair, someone told me that if I wanted to stay married that I should get over it.

If anyone wanted to get over it, it was me. Yes, please to not feeling like I was going to die every day. I'd have taken that option any day of the week.

What I did next was what I call the Cirque du Soleil move.

I am not naturally part of the contortionist group but I likened my "just get over it" experience to wearing a pair of nylons backwards, twisting myself up and then locking myself and my very big bunch of feelings into a chest for a couple of weeks at a time so I could try to feel normal and not let all the feels spill out.

I worked hard only to BURST out of this extremely distressing box, like a crazy Jack in the Box person. I couldn't control my feelings and I couldn't just move on.

I felt so ashamed.

I'd feel so horrible about my behaviour and then I'd retreat back to the contorted position in my *box* again.

I was overwhelmed and desperately wanted to feel normal.

What was my problem?

If I wanted to keep my family and my marriage together, I had to get over this shit, and fast.

I thought there was something wrong with me.

This behaviour was not making me any more appealing to my spouse at the time and my *competition* still felt strong.

I felt like a freakin' disaster.

Until I found out the truth. I didn't have to get "over" anything. I didn't HAVE to do anything. No one in their right mind would choose to stay in pain and misery, but we have to be with our pain to move through it and be as whole as possible on the other side.

We have to feel it to heal it.

We're all looking for the magic pill that will take pain, struggle, tough emotions, and brutal thoughts away. Tuck those puppies away. PLEASE.

You don't get over it. You move through it.

And whatever stays with you is learning and growth and, perhaps always, some residual grief. Moving through it is painful and hard.

If we numb or avoid the dark emotions, we also lose our capacity to feel the emotions we long for more of like joy, love, happiness, peace. The list is long. No feels. No Joy.

When my mom died, I got "over" it fast.

I remember driving down a road with my three-month-old baby in the back seat thinking, what happens if you don't grieve? Do people still turn out OK?

150

My dad was a mess, my husband was struggling, I had a wee baby who was still feeding every two hours and I was going back to school full-time (disadvantage of having a baby when you are also one). I had to wrap this grief-thing up fast.

SO, I bottled everything up and moved ahead.

Brené Brown says, "When you numb the dark, you numb the light," meaning that if we numb the hard emotions, we have less capacity for the emotions we long for like happiness, joy, excitement, even love. No one wants that. I can see how that happened to me over the years. I felt content, grateful and love, but not to the extent I feel them now that I have worked through the painful feelings of my past.

You will move past this pain when you give it the time it's asking for. How long is that? I don't know. That timing varies for everyone. The first thing you can give yourself is permission to take all the time you need.

What is something that's happened to you and that you still struggle with?

How is that situation still impacting you?

Be super kind to yourself. Be self-compassionate. The more you beat yourself up about how you feel, the longer and more painful this will be. It's like self-empathy.

• Talk to yourself like you would a child who's suffering. Start with saying to yourself, "This hurts so much."

• Don't judge the experience of your pain or how you're handling it. It matters and it's painful.

• Know that everyone suffers, and your struggle deserves the space to be honoured.

• Identifying what emotion you're feeling can help too. That gives you *psychological air*, some space to experience what you're feeling. Most people can only identify three emotions: sad, happy, and angry. Increasing your emotional literacy, by being able to identify the emotion you're feeling is extremely helpful. Just naming the emotion can provide you with about 25 per cent relief in your current moment of anguish.

Then lay all this madness in a bowl of trust. You can do this. Trust that.

You're strong, and the strongest of the strong feel the pain and grief and shed more tears than most.

You may always feel a pang of pain over whatever has you on your knees right now but trust me, you haven't been brought this far to stay on the floor.

You will stand again, and the scars will remind you of how far you've come.

So much love for you in the meantime.

Reflections

Think of where you are right now in this situation and take the time to write your own *Hero* story. Yes, you're the hero.

Write freely about how you have overcome pain and what strengths in your character have helped you move through this massive mess.

Who have you become at the end of your new story?

How have you helped others as a result of moving through this hardship?

How does this help you with what you've been struggling with?

Chapter 42 (P/R)

When You're Face Down

Never lie to me.

That's the one thing people who know me, know I will not tolerate.

Don't tell me half-truths. Don't be anything less than boldly transparent or I feel blown back by betrayal.

I stand for truth and transparency and have experienced betrayal, so I am also keenly aware of the triggers that run alongside my values.

So, when I was lied to recently, by some people I love dearly, I felt blindsided. I was questioning my relationship with these people. When I pointed out the lies, there was no ownership.

All of this just added to my hurt. I asked for space to see what I needed to move forward and that was met with more defensiveness and extreme discomfort.

I cried more than I have cried since I can remember. I felt like my heart weighed 1000 pounds and no matter what I did, I seeped sorrow and loss.

In my brokenness, I leaned into my integrity and while I was still spitting grit from falling flat on my face, I didn't do what seemed logical or listen to the roar of my gremlins.

When I'm feeling vulnerable I need to listen to my heart.

My heart was producing all the tears. Normally I feel angry, which helps me to move forward and not get bogged down by emotions I'm not comfortable with grief and sadness.

Even though it's hard I knew I would be in big trouble if I didn't feel these big feels, so I gave in and let the emotions move through me.

I cried and I felt tired. I felt such betrayal and longing to be seen, heard and honoured, fully knowing that may never happen.

The heart knows what we need. We so often don't heed its leadings because it feels awkward, painful, or even weird, but it's where our truth lies. Without its compass in a storm, we are likely to get off course.

I reached out to a few of my people. I shared my struggle and they loved me through it.

They saw my pain, without judgment and honoured it.

I meditated, journaled, and prayed a lot.

Sometimes you'll be face down getting your ass kicked. This was that moment for me. I don't have a more polite way to describe this although perhaps *kicked in the teeth* works. You can decide what fits.

How do we rise up? By trusting ourselves.

We have to know what's going on inside of us. So, I made extra time for quiet. We all need space to process.

I trusted my truth. I looked back at my values and defined even more clearly what they meant to me and the behaviours that supported them. This helped me stay grounded and showed me why this situation hurt me so much. It also showed what I needed to clearly communicate so we could rebuild our relationship and regain what had been lost.

Transparency was the value that was violated. I define transparency as courageous honesty, volunteering the truth.

I refined it further – telling the whole truth.

I realized that the saying, "What people don't know won't hurt them," is a flat-out lie.

I added, "If you know something that could hurt me-tell me."

Even if it hurts me, at least I won't be left in the dark or feel like I've been duped.

I filled myself with truth. I listened to audiobooks about the science of how we rise from a fall. I love Brené Brown and I may need therapy for this, but when I miss my mom, I listen to Brené as she's science and sass, just what I need. (My mom was more sandwiches and love, but I'll take what I can get.) Brené reminds me to keep moving and where I need to focus when I feel knocked down. Her book *Rising Strong* has helped me so much.

Someone in a support group that I facilitate asked me what I do for self care. I joked that I was high maintenance when it comes to self care.

I need a lot of it! Bring on even more self care.

I have a huge toolbox of tools that bolster resilience; many I practice daily. Many I've shared with you. I also spent my quiet time counting widgets. What does that mean? I was too exhausted to do challenging tasks, so I dove into simple tasks, ones that required minimal attention and whose basic rhythm soothed me. Our brains are soothed when we're suffering by simple tasks.

I got creative. As time went on and things were not getting much better, I asked myself what I needed. I realized I wanted to be creative. Not paint a Picasso or anything, just making some simple Christmas cards for my clients. It was relaxing, joy-giving, and helped me feel grounded.

I reached out and texted others who had been struggling to let them know I was thinking about them. We are never the only ones struggling and using our pain to remind us to reach out to others results in a blessing and sometimes even a joy. It gets us moving past our own troubles.

I also continued working. I LOVE working with my clients. It's such an honour and so grounding. I would do this work for free, it fills my soul to the brim, so I relished time with them.

All of these practices reinforced that the universe is oddly kind amidst the greatest of aches and there is no failing, only learning. Hearts heal, relationships change and to truly live is messy, gritty, and painful at times. I want to really live and experience all of what life brings me and, eventually, the sun does come up. I just need to wade deep into truth, lean into love and be open to see joy sprinkled into the hardest of times.

Reflections

Reflect on a recent situation that you're struggling with.

Was there a value violation? What value was violated?

Was there something from your past that made this even more painful?

What needs to be honoured from that situation that's part of your story now?

How does knowing what your core values are and what has happened in the past clarify why this was so painful?

Is there anything that you'd like to do to honour yourself in this situation?

Chapter 43 (R)

Wow Honey
That Was Amazing!

My partner and I usually end off our weekly meeting with a kiss.

Our meeting is called "The state of the union." (John Gottman, *7 Principles for Making Marriage Work*)

It's not that much different than a business meeting, to be honest. It brings our relationship front and centre, we connect, and we create a deeper understanding of how we can love and appreciate each other more deeply.

We joke that we have 43 years of combined marital experience, which sounds funny, but the heartbreak of a long relationship ending was by far the most devastating experience of my life.

I don't want it to happen again and given the second chance to love someone is truly one of the greatest gifts and I'm giving it all I have.

People define success in many ways, but I've always thought if one could build an empire and their personal lives fell apart in the meantime, something was really off. Don't get me wrong-things happen outside of our control, but if you're not balanced in your investment of time and energy in your health, your relationships and your work-there are bound to be some problems.

I invest A LOT of time and energy into intentionally building my businesses and I help others do the same. Boldly, I want it all: a healthy life, thriving businesses and a vibrant life with a long relationship with my love. I want all the things.

Are you being as intentional with your primary relationships as you are with your business or with your career?

A new relationship is extremely exciting at first and investing in it is easy, it's like loving a bite of a chocolate bar -it's yummy and delicious and how can you help but swoon over it? But by the end, it's chocolate and it's OK, but the nuts just don't crunch the way they used to.

It's like any long-term relationship. You've settled in. Oh sure, you go out on "dates" with your partner, but your water has more sparkle than your love life.

I work with dynamic business leaders and in the course of a year they have meetings with their accountants, their staff, and other strategic allies to assess how things are going. They look at where they need to switch things up to make things work more effectively in their businesses.

We rarely evaluate or put that kind of energy into our relationships. We have reviews with our staff to make sure things are going well and we provide feedback for growth. Yet we don't invest the same amount of energy into our primary relationships.

What's holding us back?

I can hear you saying, "I'm going to have a meeting with my partner and see where things are at?" Yup.

I'm precisely saying that, but unlike at work, at this meeting, you can have candles, wine, and hold hands if you'd like. This is about maintaining a love relationship and the little things DO COUNT.

When's the last time you asked your partner or even your kids what they need from you to make the relationship even stronger? On the other hand, when have you had a chance to sincerely give feedback as to what would make you thrive?

Dr. John Gottman's 40 years of research on relationships shows that 5.5 hours a week of time investment is required to have a thriving re-lationship. (Don't panic. I know you think you don't have the time, but we've talked about carving out space and flexibility. You have time!) Even start with 20 min more a week. That'd be a great start.

Take one of the tools and try it out and then you can add to it. :)

Dr. Gottman's *Magic Hours* instructions:

Weekly meetings, called the *State of the Union*, using the following for-mat: (This is scheduled like a meeting)

1.   Start by telling each other what's going well in the relationship.

2.   Tell each other five things you appreciate about each other. Try to be specific.

3.   Select an issue that may not have been resolved that you'd like to talk about.

Start gently, with "I feel" in those situations, and "I need." And go back to the previous chapter with the defense lowering technique if needed.

4.   Ask one another what you can do to make the other feel loved that week.

We also look at each other's calendars, so we know what the week is like for one another and set a time for a date or two.

More *Magic Hours* goodness:

Partings

•   Don't part in the morning without knowing one interesting thing that will happen in your partner's day. Say goodbye with a six-second kiss.

Reunions

•   Start with a six-second kiss.

•   Have a stress reducing conversation. Each take 10 minutes to "unpack" your day. Offer support and no advice. Understanding must always proceed advice.

Admiration and Appreciation

•   Find some way, everyday, to genuinely communicate affection and appreciation towards your partner.

Affection

•   Show each other lots of affection. Be playful and have fun every day.

Date

•   Weekly and in addition to doing the State of the Union, ask open-ended questions, show genuine interest, and enjoy each other.

Pick one of the above and invest in your relationship. It's worth it and without the skills to keep your relationship moving ahead, you're risking its demise.

Think this is over the top?

I get that, but like I mentioned before, Dr. Gottman can predict a couple's likelihood of divorce by watching them interact for 15 minutes. His tools have been developed and scientifically tested in order to help you avoid becoming one of his statistics.

AND you can adjust the tools to use with your kids, your family night and with your team at work. (Probably leave out the kissing part with your team ;).

Know that greetings/partings, time to connect, and appreciation is massively important in all relationships. I have corporate clients who use Dr. Gottman's framework as part of their feedback to their team members.

Love is one of the greatest gifts we can share and, like all good and delicious things, savour it and do what you can to help it flourish.

Reflections

What's one technique from those listed above that you would like to try out in your life?

Who will you do it with?

What's the next step to implement the practice?

What will a greater investment in your relationship give you?

That sounds like joy-yummmm!

Chapter 44 (M/E)

I Have a Grapefruit In My Pants

I didn't want to write about this because EVEN I'm sick of myself and my exceptional ability to grow extra bits in my body, but it's my life, my body and I'm here with what is.

I've been having some pain issues and the doctor told me that I have a big fibroid in my uterus. It's the size of a grapefruit AND my uterus is that of a three-month pregnant momma's. The doctor also mentioned I should be super grateful I can still fit in my jeans with this bugger in me and that my belly isn't bulging given what I have going on internally, and I am.

OK I know I write about tumours a lot-grateful again, this is a benign one, but it's a big bugger. While I've been researching how to treat this new grapefruit guy, as surgery (if it's an option) has a six to nine-month waiting list to even see someone about it, I have time on my hands.

This process of being uncomfortable and having to listen to what I need has taught me a lot.

I'm standing, as sitting isn't my favourite go-to move right now. The fibroid is not like a baby and not growing quite right, so sitting and I are on a break.

I was reading a gynecologist's take on fibroids and some treatments. Dr. Christiane Northrup suggested that one reflects on a few things in their lives when they have a new diagnosis, as perhaps there are areas that are not being honoured. (www.drnorthrup.com)

The questions were:

Is there anything that you would like to be more creative with in your life or long to create?

The first thing that popped into my head was writing. So, I'm writing this book in fact. AND YOU ARE HERE reading it-Thank you!! No seriously BIG thanks to you precious reader.

Writing is challenging as I worry people are sick of what I might have to say, but when we create it's not about the receiver as it so much about the creator. Whether my words get read or not, it is not my job to worry about that.

For the first four weeks, I was not allowed to exercise at all. I wasn't allowed to keep my vigorous six days a week boot camp schedule or even go on walks.

Exercising keeps me sane and lean, none of which come naturally to me. I NEED TO EXERCISE. Need to, or so I thought.

If someone had told me that I was going to be in constant pain, only to be made worse with movement and excruciating with exercise, and that I would not be able to move with ease or actually sit, I would have told them, "Call the psych ward, book me a room, because that's where I'm headed."

I need to move to feel good. It's my joy spot. It's my anti-depressant to be honest.

Yet, by an act of grace, I'm not there. Even two years later, since all of that started, and finding out that I am not a surgical candidate, I am OK. Only now can I run for a few minutes but sometimes that increases my pain intensely and I can't do anything besides walk, for a week. AND I am not there. No psych ward. I do struggle with my mental health and my body image because of the lack of intense exercise, but I'm still OK and have learned to adjust and endure more than I thought. Chronic pain can be a joy stealer, to put it mildly.

Pain is an ass kicking, joy killing slog fest. I will say that. Is it a place that you can learn more than you ever thought possible? Yes.

SO that is what the season of pain did. Pain deepened the meaning in my life, deepened the gratitude I experience and allowed for deep joy like I never knew.

I've had lots of time to think; discomfort provides plenty of space for that.

The thinking has led me to reflect on what keeps us sane.

The number one lifesaver is this:

If we're suffering, we need friends and our BFF in the mess is us. I needed to be my own BFF.

I always say we practice what we need regularly so that when we RE-ALLY need it, it comes more naturally.

I've been practicing self-compassion for years and it's CHANGED this experience of chronic pain for me. I couldn't even carry a jug of milk from my car at first and the first voice in my head was, *honey, you're OK, it won't always be like this, you're doing so well.*

The essence of self-compassion is three-fold, but I add some icing on the self-compassion cake by calling myself an endearing term. I call many people I love "Honey," so I start my self-talk with Honey because it's hard to treat yourself like a jerk when you start with a sweet name.

I use my truth statement: "I'll have exactly what I need when I need it." I moved my entire house without lifting one box. Not one box. I packed them and left them exactly where they were, and my beloved moved everyone by himself. I did have what I needed. NOT the way I wanted it. That's not always part of it.

Like a ticket for the bus, I get it when I get on the bus. Right then. Not before. I can do this. Whatever it is. Always.

Know there's grace in this space. Lean into your spiritual beliefs what-ever they may be. You believe in Mother Nature, a kind universe, a deity; you do you. Spirituality really bolsters our resilience. I believe in a kind and loving God. Not a religious thing, a pure goodness thing, like pure love, like sunshine. I feel like that allows me to walk with light shining on me in whatever I'm facing. When it feels dark around me, I have what I need and I'm not alone.

Have some fun with it, whatever life it is throwing at you. I call all my other tumours my *bits and my buddy* (the buddy is a bigger tumour on my thyroid) named affectionately by my honey.

I was leading a group of teens that share my genetic condition, in a conversation about how they manage the stress of having tumours. We were coming up with funny stories about how they got so many scars and I mentioned the new grapefruit guy, the 18-year-old beside me said, "You should name him after a frat boy because who hasn't had a frat boy try to get into their pants at least once?"

She suggested Chad.

"That's a douchey name," she said.

I laughed so hard and so Chad it is. Good news is that Chad is even shrinking. Maybe Chad isn't such a jerk after all.

Dress for how you want to feel. Dress in what makes you feel good. I am a "dresser upper." I don't own pajamas so staying in those all day is not an option and I always feel better in a blazer and done up. That's how I dress whether I see another human all day or not-it helps a lot! I also love a good fake flower on my lapel. :)

Don't give up. There is always hope. Always. Look at ways to treat, love, embrace or fight these buggers in your life. I like to swing between the two.

Try things. I found a validated study that said green tea extract can be helpful to make CHAD shrink to a more docile chad, I'm in for trying. Drinking less alcohol and eating less red meat is also supposed to be good, so I'm doing that too. I found some physio that is supposed to help relieve some of the discomfort and tension. I do movement and breath work and that beats doing nothing. Over the last couple of years, Chad the formidable fibroid, has shrunk by 30%. I'll take that!

Trust yourself. Sometimes that's as simple as laying down more and getting more rest. You know what you need. Listen to yourself.

Avoid triggers. I was going to weigh myself to see what I weighed and decided not to. Even my doctor doesn't weigh me. I am learning new ways to be with me.

The scale is rarely my friend so I'm not going near it. Avoid what doesn't serve you and can trigger more pain when you're already knee deep in it.

Ask for help. We've been through this and know it's one of my biggest challenges. I am not good at this and you might not be either. Ask anyway. I've asked people to carry things. Even a jug of milk.

No future surfing. Get off that board! All *what ifs* must be avoided. What if this doesn't get better, what if I can't stand the pain? NOPE. Not going there. If someone had told me that it would take almost two years for me to find some relief, I wouldn't have made it. I needed to take things one day at a time.

Be grateful. SOOOOO grateful. I think shadows in our lives make the bright spots more vivid. I am so grateful this is not worse, and I have a job that I can do standing or from the couch. I have a partner who loves me no matter what and he's been with me through a lot of new things. I have a great life and so many wonderful people surrounding me.

Put up boundaries. I couldn't and still can't do everything. I couldn't bend over or lift anything so even beloved JoySocks went on a break. I couldn't get the boxes filled with JoySocks down the stairs, so I stopped donating to our sites for a while and I was committed to hosting a fundraiser, so I concentrated on that. I had to let what I normally do go for a while.

I am very clear on what is OK and what is not. I create boundaries based on that information.

Trust. Everything is an opportunity to grow. I trust this isn't a waste. I trust I have what I need. I trust my body's capacity to heal.

I trust that I am loved and held and will heal.

AND for the love of pearl (southern expression, I went to college in Mississippi ;), PISS AND MOAN with perspective. The most resilient people aren't candy coating things. They complain while recognizing the reality of their situations.

While I hope you don't have a grapefruit in your pants, or aren't in chronic pain, I know we all have things that ache and sometimes the worst aches are not physical. In the midst of this, my hope is that you feel held in grace, bathed in peace, and sense a sparkle of joy to help you keep moving forward. I'm here alongside you.

Reflections

How can you be kinder to yourself right now?

What statement brings you back to the truth about how resilient you want to believe yourself to be?

What are you curious about trying that could help you?

How can you avoid future surfing?

What do you want to trust about this situation?

What triggers can you avoid?

What boundaries do you need?

Anything even mildly humorous about this situation?

Who can you piss and moan to? When will you do that?

Chapter 45 (E)

Comfortably Numb

I'm a number.

Not a numBer, as in a numerical digit. A Numb'er' pronounced, num-mer.

I engage in behaviours that cause me to be distracted by things that contribute to me not feeling or living fully.

Are you a number too?

I work from home. I am an extrovert, and I am alone most of the day. My top value is connection. I am alone most of the day (did I mention that?). I have client calls over the phone but in between them, I often end up on social media.

There's nothing wrong with social media. I LOVE people and I love staying connected to people, BUT the problem arises when we aren't intentional about a certain behaviour and it starts to not serve our highest good.

I was journaling the other day and I asked myself what was keeping me from feeling purposeful. Were there any habits that I engaged in that took away my feeling of purposefulness?

The first thing I thought of was how often, when I want a wee break during the day, I go to social media.

I do it without thinking.

I realized that I was using social media as a way to connect, which is good EXCEPT I get caught up in a rabbit hole of feeds and articles, you name it. All of a sudden, 20 minutes is gone, not once, but twice and more honestly probably four or five times a day.

WHAT THE HECK?!?-that's 80 to 100 minutes of my life that I am trying to feel connected, missing the mark after about five minutes and not even really aware of where the time goes.

That's numbing.

Damn it. I DO NOT WANT TO BE A NUMBER.

When we numb the dark feelings like loneliness or disconnection from people or purpose, we also numb the feelings we love, like joy (need I say more!), love, and contentment.

I knew something was up when I woke up in the night feeling like something was off. Not in my body so much as in my heart. I felt blah, unfocused, and not on purpose. Things felt grey.

In the morning, I explored the feeling with my coach and realized I was numbing. Confirmed the diagnosis. Dammit.

The numbing agent - social media.

It was helping me avoid making some hard decisions around relationships and avoid some business development projects.

Social media was my distraction, my way of filling time to keep from filling it with purposeful things like writing, revamping some programs I've built and focusing on what's in line with my values and serving a bigger purpose. Social media was my shadow comforter.

In her book *The Life Organizer*, Jennifer Louden writes, "Shadow comforts can take any form. It's not what you do; it's *why* you do it that makes the difference. You can eat a piece of chocolate as a holy wafer of sweetness- a real comfort-or you can cram an entire chocolate bar into your mouth without even tasting it in a frantic attempt to soothe yourself- a shadow comfort."

It's not what you do that's the issue, it's why you do it.

Yesterday I hid my social media apps on my phone. I caught myself several times in the morning when I was alone, grabbing my phone to go "there." Damn this habit!

Checking social media was an unconscious habit and I imagine I've been like this for a while and never noticed until I talked and journaled about it. I feel shame when I think about where I've wasted time away.

Brené Brown says in her book, *Daring Greatly*, the most accurate answers to the question about what drives numbing and sounds more like the answers to, "What's your sign?" (How romantic.)

Anxiety with shame rising.

Disconnection with shame rising.

Anxiety and disconnection with shame rising.

Turns out my sign is: *Scorpio with an acute fear of disconnection so I create connection by constantly going on social media so I can avoid feeling lonely.*

Brené continues, when I interviewed the research participants (whom I'd describe as living a wholehearted life) about numbing, they consistently talked about three things:

1. Learning how to feel their feelings.

2. Staying mindful about numbing behaviors (they struggled too).

3. Learning how to lean into the discomfort of hard emotions.

Here's my unpacking in case it helps you unpack your own challenges more.

1.   I do feel alone a lot. That feels achy and isolating at times. Sometimes I feel left out. My lack of connection is not just about people, its also about not connecting with what I feel I'm being led to do. I have some projects I want to pursue, but I realize now that shame's message of, 'Who do you think you are?' keeps me from pursuing them and social media numbs me enough that I get off track and avoid my more purposeful work.

It's hard to write these things, never mind feel them. I also know they're feelings. I feel alone, but it's not always an accurate reflection of the truth in my life; it's a, "go to."

I also realize that I used to go to a gym I LOVED everyday and I got to be with people and exercise which helped my mental health so much. However, I can no longer do that which has led to more isolation. So, I ache for more connection. Of course, I would feel off right now. Better to feel it and be with it then numb that loss.

2.   I numb with social media. (I feel like I'm in a support group meeting and that's probably a good thing)

I numb with research rather than getting things done, overusing my value of learning.

I numb with extreme discipline. I love that feeling, or that feeling loves me (relationship status: complicated)

I probably numb with wine on occasion. A glass is a holy vessel of yum, but 2 or 3, not so much.

3.   Feeling those hard emotions, saying them, or writing them, helps

to clearly identify them and even helps to reduce their charge. It's called emotional literacy. So, I'm working on being more literate. I am getting better and am getting accustomed to leaning in, not numbing away. I'm allowing myself to notice when I feel lonely, disconnected, and feel blah and out of tune with myself. That's a start to what's going on behind the scenes.

I've added some of my own tools to refine the above strategies.

Identify what behaviours can be implemented to reinforce the connection or feelings you long for.

Instead of going on social media, connect with people via text. Nothing long or extravagant but purposeful. A holy wafer of connection.

Think about what you need to feel connected to your deeper purpose and give that attention.

Writing does that and so do walks with friends.

For me, that includes naps as well. Tired Leona is easily distracted and more likely to numb. 20 minutes a day, saves me every time.

Reflect on anything you need to do differently to be more connected to what really matters.

The truth is, this all stings a little; OK a lot. But the GIFT of fully living is so worth it and I don't want to miss a thing. My guess is that you don't either. Get curious: where do you numb? There's no shame here. We all do it and when we shine a light on it, it can't help but to dissolve. That's where the goodness shows up. That's a joy spot.

Reflections

When do you feel purposeful?

What distracts you from doing more of that?

How do you numb?

What does the numbing give you?

What self care do you need that would bring you comfort?

What will you do differently to stop numbing and start living more purposefully?

Chapter 46 (P)

Those Rotten Bananas

I feel fear. I feel doubt. I feel angry. I feel hurt.

I don't like those feelings. I don't want to be with those feelings.

I'd like to pick out my feelings for the day, like I'm picking fruit from a basket. Take the ones I like and leave the black bananas, extra soft oranges, or super bruised apples of hard feelings behind.

Someone ELSE can throw them in the compost bin when I walk away from the fruit basket of emotions. If I must, I will make muffins from those crappy bananas, but my classic move is to freeze those suckers and not deal with them until they fall out of the freezer. I've been doing that for my whole life.

I have been having little luck in trying to solve my pain issues no matter what I do. Recently, I was told by my doctor that surgery will not alleviate my pain, as the source of my pain is tight muscles, like a tight jaw. This doesn't clear up easily. Pain can form a loop in our brains. The pain etches grooves into our brain and any stimulus becomes associated with it and brings on more pain.

I set up an appointment with a trauma therapist to see if there was anything psychologically associated with the pain I was feeling. I was scared, thinking that there might be something ominous that I had blocked out of my memory from my childhood.

What became very evident in the therapy session was that I was filled with emotions that I had never dealt with – predominantly grief, sadness, and sorrow.

My freezer was stuffed full of black bananas.

I don't like those rotten bananas.

I really don't like all of those "wet" emotions. The mascara ruining and puffy eye bringing emotions. AT All. I don't really do sadness. I've mentioned that a thousand times before. I feel like if I jump into that well I'll drown. It really surprised me how much sadness was showing up with my therapist's gentle expertise and guidance.

The well was deep and filled with tears.

I know I don't do sadness well. I remember when my kids were young, and I'd hear my friends talk about feeling overwhelmed and they would cry. I would think about how I never felt close to tears.

I would feel pissed off and determined to push through whatever shit show I was facing. Looking back, I had every reason to be overwhelmed. I ran a day home, had my own little kids and no car. At one point, I had five children, four-and-under. My partner worked 60-70 hours a week. I don't remember much of that time. Probably for the best; small mercies perhaps. Maybe I was a wimp, which we will swing around to later.

The other piece I realized was how much I had carried other people's stuff. I carried things and took responsibility for things that were not mine. Often and despite suffering myself, I had set aside my feelings to care for others. Often to my demise.

When my mom died, I was 22, with a newborn. I felt overwhelmed. I packed that pain down deep. Hoping it would never resurface.

I hear the sadness gremlin whisper and sneer at my words.

"You're fine," she says. "You were an adult, don't make a mountain out of a molehill." What is a molehill anyways? It was such a common phrase used in our house to suck it up and soldier through.

So, your mom died, big deal.

That gremlin is a bastard because she makes me minimize everything.

Sometimes there is no other choice but to move on when we are faced with tough emotions. Like we would when dealing with a suffering child. I can't set aside my role as a mother to say, "I know you're struggling, but I need to tap out for a while and process my own feelings."

That's not realistic.

Here I was in the therapist's office, crying so hard for all the sadness I'd locked away. I realized how excruciatingly I missed my mom. I knew I missed her on her birthday but had no idea how much I ached for her, as

I felt during that session. I tried not to think about her. Another indication of my numbing.

Don't think, just move on.

As I noticed my sadness, there were sensations associated with it evident in my body. My shoulders did feel heavy and almost numb, my pain intensified even more from when I came in. I felt so heavy.

There was also my inner voice saying, "You're fine, this isn't the worst thing." Which apparently, as I blubbered my way through the session, I said several times. Hedging my pain as I went.

I have minimized my sadness over my entire life. Maybe you have too.

When sadness came up, I would stuff it and tell myself, "It's not so bad. So many others have had it far worse."

Even now I'm feeling like a wimp for thinking anything I've been through has been all that bad.

I mask my sadness or any type of wet feelings with "soldiering on" or "no time for this," or "you're fine," or I'd pick another emotion, like anger, to get a move on.

You know I was not modelled healthy sadness. I only saw my mom get sad once. My dad, on the other hand, was often overwhelmed by sadness and that came with a terrifying consequence for me and lots of opportunity to shoulder his pain. If I cried, he would cry more and lean on me. I couldn't bear his weight when I was already struggling. So, I stuffed mine.

The therapist told me that when I minimized my stories or told myself minimizing comments, that I needed to take them as my invitation to feel instead.

As our session approached an end, I asked my therapist what I could do to process all that sadness outside of her care and move through it.

Let's be clear, if I was honest, I wanted the "emotional processing your stuff" fast-track program, preferably online, pain-free and completed with a certification in accelerated emotional processing. As a bonus, a keto lollipop. Please. Turns out, there's no such program. The only way I can get "over this" is by moving through the wetness. Shit.

I had to work on being with the wet emotions and the minimizing comments. They were my invitations, without judgment, to allow more space for the feelings. My job was to feel more. Dammit.

The learning for me is clear and I don't want to keep being a stuffer or a minimizer or a number. Unprocessed emotions do not lay dormant, they fester and show up somehow at some point. So, I've been doing the work to feel.

What helps me is writing about points in my life and feeling some of the feelings. The sadness doesn't bubble up easily and that's OK. It does allow me to see some of my patterns and coping mechanisms.

I am doing my best to honour myself the way I am.

What I do know: I am aware of the feelings I am not comfortable with.

What I do to avoid them: pick secondary feelings like anger or get busy doing "urgent" things, leaving little space for the feelings.

So, I'm choosing things like:

Leave space to feel the feeling more fully.

Give myself permission to feel the feels.

Don't compare my story with other's.

Notice where I minimize my past.

Provide opportunities to feel sadness.

This has been the "best" part: I cried my face off watching some TV shows, sometimes because of sadness, but sometimes for intense joy. (I may have even clapped for the goodness.)

Here's the thing with processing sorrow. Crying is very good for you. Crying is soap for the soul.

Crying releases emotions AND I don't have to be thinking of my own losses to have the crying be effective (bring on the sad movie suggestions). It all helps with the unstuffing. It's good to cry and I'm proud of myself for letting myself really cry. And this is the closest I will get to my fast track program so I will take it!

I have had a great life with some really gritty parts and, whether those parts of my story would impact you as they have me, is not my business.

Experiences in my life have weighed me down and my way home has been me taking the time to honour their impact on my life-and they do deserve to be honoured, just like yours do. This creates more room for joy.

We increase our capacity for joy by feeling the feelings we maybe less fond of. This is good news.

They are my story, my shadows, and my sorrows. I want to be free of the weight of that history in the best way possible and that way is through the fruit basket of feelings. I'm acknowledging the black bananas and mouldy oranges in order to experience more of the delicious goodness I desire more of. I want more space for joy to seep in. I imagine you do too.

What are your Bananas?

Reflections

What emotions do you struggle *being* with?

What were you told or modelled when you were a child about those feelings?

What are the gremlins you have around experiencing those tough emotions? What are their messages?

How do those hold you back?

What causes you to stuff the tough emotions?

What would it look like to give more space to experiences that you have been through and that still weigh you down?

What would you like to honour?

What permission do you want to give yourself to allow for more grace and space as you dive in?

What will you do to honour those rough times?

What's your best possible outcome for having moved through what feels like a mess?

Chapter 47 (E)

Party Pooper

No effing way!"

Even I was caught off guard with what I'd spat out. My honey looked shocked and I was equally shocked as I let the *pissedoffness* fly out of me from some unknown source. Youch!

We were sitting in a restaurant and my love was suggesting who we should personally reach out to and invite to the JoySocks Party I would be hosting in a few months. My immediate response was, "Eff that, it's enough work, I'm not inviting specific people. They'll see it on the Facebook event invite. If they want to come, great; if not, I DON'T CARE."

What was that?

The moment felt like when you're having an argument someone and then you bring up something you've been hurt about since 1975. It felt deep and tasted bitter as I spat it out.

It took a couple of minutes for me to feel normal again.

I thought- *what was that?*

My beloved's face clearly reflected a similar sentiment. (Poor lamb.)

When I feel an emotional charge, it's my invitation to get curious. (AND yours too.)

In the past, I would have stuffed the feelings down soooo deep and, after apologizing to the person who experienced it with me and tried not to think of it again. In this case, I apologized as I had snapped at my beloved for no apparent reason and then gently looked at what was going on.

Resentment is most often a signal of a lack of boundaries. CLEAR-LY, I was a tad resentful and thus in need of some boundaries. Crap.

Brené Brown provides a framework for establishing boundaries and labels it as Living BIG. (Brené Brown, *Rising Strong*)

Boundaries. Integrity. Generosity.

Here are the basics:

What boundaries do I need in order to live generously with myself and others while living according to my values? Integrity in the framework is simply defined as what's OK and not OK, your values make that clear.

SO clearly something wasn't OK. AND I wasn't living with good boundaries.

The truth was, JoySocks needed to raise money to run and we started the birthday party idea to be an annual party to honour JoySocks and use it as a means to raise funds. There was a group of people who were going to take it on. We started planning and then they were unable to help, so it ended up being me taking it on with a legion of volunteers. They were amazing, but it was not what I had anticipated. It was so much work. Work I'm not that good at and find very stressful.

There are a million details that go on behind the scenes of an event. Anyone who knows me knows that details and filling out forms and tedious crap KILLS ME!

We raised a ton of money the first year, but I was exhausted for a week after. Still, we continued annually because it seemed like a good idea, only to dread it the next year. That year I didn't dread it because I was in a new, fresh frame of mind where I refuse to dread anything, however when the resentment bubbled up, I knew things needed to change.

I DISLIKE (hate may not be too strong of a word), planning complex events.

I once planned a surprise party for my love and 50 invited guests, which didn't require me to fill out a six-page liquor licence application, or a six-page health services food service permission form, or contact the police department, or email the fire department, or get insurance… I think you get the point. I threw that baby together in a few hours and it was great.

That was a party, not an event with 3000 things that have to happen behind the scenes to make it work. I may be exaggerating about the 3000 moving parts, but only by three things, maybe.

Did you know you have to serve two kinds of protein when you have booze at a party where you are raising money? AND the health department must know exactly what they are, what store you're buying them from and what forms of protein you are serving? And did you know that you must charge a certain amount per ounce of alcohol served? There's a math equation in here people! These details are my death.

You can see I still have some issues to work through… :)

So, if I wanted to live with integrity and not dread what was going on in my life, I needed to change some things up. I decided that night; it would be the last JoySocks bday party we'd have.

Don't get me wrong; I've been infinitely grateful for everyone who has come to the event, for the INCREDIBLE volunteers who have carried this event, and for all the success we have had, and so many more things. SO GRATEFUL!!

I just couldn't do another one. I'd be gritting my teeth and I hadn't come this far for that.

Here's what happened next.

Shame. I can smell her from a mile away.

I caught her in her tracks. She had two messages, that sneaky vixen, "You're not enough," and "Who do you think you are?"

I lessened her grip by talking with my beloved and he showed me empathy, which helped lessen the drip of shame. He said, "I know how hard this is, every year I see it."

Damn that felt good, like salve on a wound.

I followed with self-compassion, *shit this is hard, you've been struggling,* I thought to myself.

From here, I could be kind to myself and dip a toe into the "being generous with myself" pond.

So, if I were going to be generous with myself, understanding there's nothing wrong with me for not being an event planner, I'd change things up.

Integrity for me is the truth of what's OK and what's not OK. If planning this event was truly OK for me, why did it feel so awful? Because it wasn't OK. It was a good idea at the time but now that I knew better, I would do better.

What's OK- is to have an event.

What's OK - is that said venue must come with its own food and licensing, Yes! (is it just me or did you hear some angels sing?)

What's OK - an event where I can actually connect with people and have fun with them-YES PLEASE!

What's not OK - is doing it right after my birthday so my inner five-year-old birthday girl starts to die after said birthday.

What's not OK - is an event where there are so many moving parts.

What's not OK - events for JoySocks that suck the joy out of every bit of the founder's marrow while planning the event. NOPE.

Even now, I can feel shame crawl up my back. I worry about what you'll think as you read this. Like I'm some horrible person. I think kindly to myself, *you're not horrible, honey, you just can't stay within integrity and keep doing things this way.*

What would be horrible would be realizing how this wasn't working for me and pushing through for the next decade, regardless. It was too late to change things that year but with the warning shot of resentment, I switched things up and decided that, when we need more money for JoySocks, we won't throw another party.

Hallelujah!

Let's leave the resentments behind and courageously step into freedom.

It will take courage and great boundaries by determining what's OK and what's not, but you can do that.

Some boundaries and self-kindness will help you live more fully in your boundaries and that's where the freedom and joy live!!! I want some of that!!

I hope you switch things up too.

Reflections

What are you tolerating in your life?

What's one thing that pops up or, at times, creeps in with a seething kind of rage or, even slightly more terrifying, leads you to numb out those feelings?

What's OK and what's not OK with the places you feel resentful?

What boundaries will you put in place to live in line with your values?

Reach out if you need help :) at findingyourjoyspot.com (I'm not joking).

Chapter 48 (P)

I'm Pissed Off

And now I'm not.

I get angry often, but having said that, I rarely ACT angry. I can't recall the last time I even raised my voice.

When my kids were little, I would feel angry at having little sleep, at my house being a mess, at feeling tried and wrung out, and I took it as a sign that I should just keep motoring on-so I kept busy, only noticing that I felt angry after a night of no sleep. Since I couldn't do anything about it, I just kept moving.

Lately I have been working on being more mindful of my anger. SO much emotional baggage to work through. (Beloved reader-thanks for sticking with me!) I don't know why my go-to emotion is anger, the emotion that sets me off, and not sadness or anything else. Mostly it's anger that rises up and then subsides. Guess it just is.

When I get angry, I notice it in my body. My chest gets tight and it feels like my blood pressure increases and sometimes my heart beats faster.

While anger is often directed at others, it has been my reminder for me to focus inward, like a bratty feeling two-year-old needing some attention while it has a melt-down on my "emotional kitchen floor."

Do you find yourself getting angry? Are you aware of what triggers it?

Some of the inquiry that helps me receive my much-needed messages are:

1. Is there a value violation here?

Our values are who we intrinsically are. When someone else does something that is outside of our values, we can feel angry. I zero in on what value is being violated.

I have a real value around respect. When someone treats me in a way that makes me feel like I wasn't respected, I get angry. Add in a lack of kindness (another value) and I see red!

My "job" is not to discharge my flurry of feelings on them. My job is to recognize that I am triggered, ask if I need to do anything and, only if I've processed this moment, am I able to act within my own values.

Sometimes I just walk away. Think of someone cutting you off in parking lot and then giving you the finger. I don't need to stop the person to have a conversation about that.

2. Am I blaming someone else for something and feeling *judgy* and like flinging my crap onto someone else? (Youch.)

Blame is how we discharge our own pain. Perhaps we didn't ask for something we needed or hold someone accountable for something that we did ask for.

It's a tough one, but it is worth circling back and seeing if there's something that needs to be addressed; a want/need that wasn't expressed or a boundary that requires some reinforcement. Circle back to yourself or another person perhaps.

3. Is there a misunderstanding? What if you misinterpreted someone else's intention about something?

This is where you get curious rather than critical.

What it could look like is saying, "I thought we had made some plans for the weekend, but I haven't heard from you and was wondering what happened?"

AHHHHHHH this feels, spacious, generous, and non-judgmental and opens the door for a conversation that will shed some light on a situation and allow for designing how you might do things differently next time.

4. Are you mad at yourself?

If something hasn't gone well, it's a great opportunity for learning and adjusting your sails.

Remember to talk to yourself like you would a friend who is struggling. Be kind to yourself in this process.

Beating yourself up takes the gooey, thinking, creative part of your brain offline and makes you more reactive and myopic in focus.

If your brain is anything like mine, you need the best parts of it to be running on all cylinders or the whole system could go to crap. Some days I can barely identify my own offspring in a line-up, I don't need my brain function to deteriorate even further.

This skill is called self-compassion. It can be learned AND the more self-compassionate one is, the better their self-confidence is as well. (Good news is you learned it or were reminded of it a few chapters back).

5. You're pissed off. PERIOD.

Perhaps this is where some self care comes in. Answer these questions, without editing:

What do I want more of?

What do I need?

What do I want less of?

Take those answers and get on it.

Hire someone to clean your house or do your taxes, go take a bath, go for a walk, take yourself out for coffee, go to the zoo; listen to what you long for more of and schedule it in.

When we feel stretched thin, wrung out and packed full, that's the perfect fertilizer for resentment to grow.

6. Is the anger hiding another emotion?

Anger is considered a secondary emotion. Anger is usually covering up another emotion. What emotion is underneath the anger?

This may require some softening and mindfulness towards the feeling of being angry. Go for a short walk, talk it out with a friend or journal and try to observe the anger, like it is outside of yourself. See if there's sadness, frustration, or disappointment underneath it.

Even simply recognizing and naming the emotion goes a long way to diffuse it.

Feeling angry is, in the end, a gift. It's a wee high-octane messenger that's trying to get us to listen more deeply to what we want and need.

The next time you feel angry, look inside for its message. It may turn out to be more of a friend than a foe. :)

What pisses you off?

Reflections

Is there a value violation that's contributing to your anger?

Are you blaming someone else for something and feeling *judgy*?

Is there a misunderstanding?

What if you misinterpreted someone else's intention about something?

What's your most generous interpretation of the person or situation?

Are you mad at yourself?

Answer these questions, without editing:

What do I want more of?

What do I need?

What do I want less of?

Take those answers and get on it.

Is the anger hiding another emotion?

Chapter 49 (P)

The Problem With JOY

After five years of dating, my honey and I decided to move in together. Yes, it's true, we had been dating for awhile, and no, we didn't live together. We weren't engaged and had taken our love life with the most delicate strategy to move things VERY slowly.

I was getting super excited about our plans, but I was having MAS-SIVE joy issues. Foreboding joy to be exact. What's that? It's the dark side of this thing I've been throwing around called joy.

I was thinking of where we would set things up in the house (have I mentioned that I LOVE DECORATING?!) and he loves everything I do, so this is even better. But I had a thought that stopped me in my tracks.

Wait for it-

What if I die before I get a chance to live with him?

WTF

I am healthy, not on any terminal protocol besides the one we are all on, with an inevitable expiry date. Chances are I will be here. As in an extreme probability.

So, what's up?

Joy has got a dark side.

Joy's got some dark spots.

Sorry.

It can be foreboding.

Joy is one of the most vulnerable emotions. I'm almost regretting picking joy as one of my favourite emotions at this point.

Joy can be so good at times that we have this GUSH of goodness and in the next moment, because of the vulnerability that it brings with it, we feel a doomsday message, a crazy message.

Like the *I'm dying* thing.

The foreboding piece of joy can keep us from feeling the goodness of it.

We avoid celebrating things like business deals, promotions, and all sorts of successes because it can reinforce the foreboding.

The key is not to avoid the joy; the celebrations, the honouring, the goodness of knowing joy more deeply.

When it's intense, it is foreboding. It's like with most people and them having middle names. It just is. It's common and it's just part of us.

First name Joy, middle name Foreboding.

We risk missing out on joy because we want to avoid the intense vulnerability of it.

When I took my oldest home from the hospital, I looked at her while she was sleeping and my next thought was, *how do we protect her from dying of SIDS?* She hadn't even been home for an hour.

Sometimes we give into the foreboding part to prepare ourselves, in some odd way, for the impending end. We don't get too attached to people or things because it feels too good to be true.

People who have been through tragedy and had dress rehearsed for it, expecting the worst, do not have an easier time when devastation hits. It's the opposite, they wish they had squeezed out all the goodness and deliciousness from joy. They wish they had lived and loved more fully.

We need joy. It's the light in our lives that gives us the fuel to keep going in the darkest of times.

Once we know joy and its sidekick, we can *lock* those intense moments of joy and the doomsday cries that sometimes accompany those moments with, drum roll please.

Gratitude.

So, when I look at the new throw pillows that I adore and a man who loves me and supports me so much, and then worry I will die, I think of what I am grateful for so that I can experience the joy we were all made for and come back to the present moment.

When is joy so intense for you that it makes you weak in the knees?

Reflections

When have you felt joy that was so intense that it made you feel afraid of something going wrong?

What were the thoughts going through your head?

What could you have been grateful for that might have helped you to savour that moment?

What brings you joy now?

How will you practice gratitude around those joy spots to lock in that joy and enjoy it even more?

Chapter 50 (E/M)

I'm Not Normal

I'm becoming more acutely aware that I'm not normal and it bothers me. Sometimes.

I do things differently than most people, or at least that's how I feel.

I feel alone when I have these feelings and I wonder what's wrong with me.

I told my love a few years back that I didn't want to have a conventional relationship when I felt like he wanted one. When I consider climbing the ladder of life together, doing the *right* things in the right order at the right time, I felt stifled and off. I thought to myself, *what's wrong with you?*

Why aren't you normal?
I thought it was because I had done the ole *been there done that* song and dance; so not doing that again.

Maybe that was part of it, but the more I explore and the more that I talk to people who also don't feel normal, I realize I am so much more like them.

I heard a friend say, "I often think I'm too weird."

I reassured her I've already won that prize so not to worry. She seems so normal. I wish I were more like her, yet she worries too.

What is this?

In the last decade, I've spent most of my time in what I liken to coming awake. I don't remember going to sleep. I think I was born somewhat awake. I remember times of deep joy, lots of fun play and feeling love so deep I would get choked up even thinking about something like telling my parents I loved them.

Then slowly I think I was lulled into a kind of sleep where I spent my days floating along learning the rules to "fit in."

I climbed the "ladder," went to school, had friends, notes were passed, cruelty was cast, new friends were made, and meanwhile, I floated along bumping into good and bad along the way, desperately hoping to fit in.

Culture played a role in creating my normalcy. I come from a traditional immigrant family. Marry young, stay home, and raise babies. I can't really imagine doing those things in that way, again, if I had a chance for a do-over.

I married young (YOUNG-21) stayed home for a time and raised kids. Birth was natural and babies were breastfed, which is all good, but not when it's not a conscious choice, in the sense that it felt like this is just what you do. Check off the boxes of a normal life. I didn't think about other options. You do what you feel like you're supposed to do. It feels normal, it feels OK, but is it really?

I started my career later in life; I put many things that I would have loved to do on hold, in order to try to fit in with the norms I was surrounded by.

I don't know how things might have changed had I done less floating and more swimming away from some norms. I think I would have been more inclined to swim upstream or perhaps in a different direction.

Because I'm not normal. I'm no longer traditional or conventional. That makes me feel like I don't fit in.

I go out with friends who have paid their children's way in life, bought their clothes, paid their bills, put them through school and I think, damn. I didn't do that with my kiddos.

I often wonder if I'm a bad person for that. Do I even fit in?

I have always believed that we learn by what we allow others to live through. I've worried that by making everything easy for our kids, they'll just glide along and won't know how to navigate regular life. I didn't want that for my kids.

I believe grit creates an opportunity for growth, so grit it is-am I a bad mom? I often wonder. Perhaps I should have used the money I didn't spend on their education for a follow-up therapy fund. There's still time.

My middle child came home after a week into her first year of university and said, "Do you want to know how many kids are paying their entire tuition on their own?"

I was intrigued to learn some new stat, so I asked, "How many?"

She said, "One. You're having dinner with her."

She was then corrected by her sister, "No, I'm the only OTHER one."

Shit, I will never get the mom of the year award.

In my relationship with my partner, my abnormality shows up and is reflected on people's faces when we used to be asked where we live. We both said our neighborhood's name, then say we both live there, in separate houses, 90 seconds away from each other, after five years of being together.

People remind us that it is expensive to be managing two households (always pulls on this Dutch girl's frugal heart/budget strings). These couples will then, tell us how they dated for six months, a year, 18 months and were waking up together each and every day.

Ya, not for us.

I'm not normal. (My beloved is totally normal, have no fear-it's me.)

People get engaged. If you're reading this right now and you have a massive diamond on your left hand-bless you. That's a great choice for you, and you're worthy of wearing that blessed ring, and this isn't a judgment of you. But even when considering going down the lifelong union road-I do not do engagement rings, I do not do solitaires.

I don't because, you guessed it, I'm not normal. People get so excited to look at the ring when all I can think of is that soooo much could be done with that money and I would do it differently.

Not because I am better than anyone else, because you know the drill by now.

I AM NOT NORMAL.

I don't like to do things because they've been done a certain way. Perhaps because I've been blind and sleepy and now, I'm not so much. Yet I feel like there's something wrong with me and, if I didn't feel like I was swimming in a different stream than a lot of people, this might feel easier.

When I was very little, I went through the annoying "why?" phase. My mom told me that my dad had a hard time on long car rides with me because I asked why without taking a break. I'm back there.

I'm back in that phase. I take things that I've always done, always believed in and I take a closer look and ask "why?"

It's been eye-opening and uncomfortable, and it's led me to feel unbearably abnormal at times.

As I sit here and write this, I know a few things that help me feel normal.

We all have our values and we've talked about how they do not always align with others. We are all unique in our values and the behaviours that reinforce them. My value of resourcefulness (spend resources wisely, save where you can so you can spend where you want) is a HUGE force in how I live my life and that shows up in many behaviours.

Independence is another massive value for me-standing on my own, doing things in a way that feels authentic and not like everyone else. Even after moving in and later getting married (and no, we didn't get engaged, and we had a surprise wedding which felt abnormal and awesome). I LOVE that we don't share bank accounts or credit cards.

Resilience is also something that's especially important and that's why I've made the parental choices I have. I like to think if there's an apocalypse, my children and I would manage all that OK (I am exaggerating but you get the point).

We all feel like we are abnormal in some ways. It's the oldest emotional affect in the book. It's the "I'm not enough" message.

Damn shame. Here it is again.

We fear that we are intrinsically flawed, and it makes us feel like we are separate from others.

ABNORMAL.

We all desperately long to fit in when what we really need is to belong. Belong to a few people who love us as we are (abnormally so), understand what drives us and what values lead the way in our lives.

I hear it with clients, "I'm supposed to or I should be doing it this way, but it seems off, gritty, crappy, inauthentic."

The norm is not working for them and to step outside of that is pure bravery and feels like a huge risk. I so get that I'm trying to live that way too.

I am convinced we all have these pieces of us that make us feel like we don't fit in, that if only we could change this one piece, we would feel more ease. We might feel normal. That would feel heavenly for me some days.

If we are true to ourselves, truly genuine, we might feel abnormal at times. It comes with being our authentic selves. It's the magic of being unique and showing up exactly as we are.

To live authentically, in line with our values and the truth of who we are, we will always feel slightly abnormal.

I use some permissions to help me move ahead and soften my *weirdness*.

Permissions will always soften a shitty *should* and help create some ease.

These are some of mine:

Permission to do things my way.

Permission to think differently than others.

Permission to try something innovative.

At the core it is really our uniqueness that adds colour to the world, and which makes the world a more beautiful place. Know that.

Get in tune with your own kind of uniqueness, awesomeness, and not-normalness. The more we know about ourselves, the more we can be fully us. That's a massive joy spot. Joy is the Journey of you. That's J.O.Y.

Reflections

Where do your "I'm not normal" gremlins show up?

What are their messages?

How do they hold you back from what really matters to you?

What could you give yourself permission for, to step closer to what really matters to you?

Who would you be if you worried less about fitting in?

Chapter 51 (P/E)

I Hated Her

Let's be clear. At first, I wanted to kill her, drive over her if I ever saw her, and let her know how she had almost killed me.

She was my former husband's affair partner. She was also young and beautiful (I'd stalked her Facebook like a rabid grade 8 girl, I'm human after all ;) I knew all of this was true.

I received an email from her that said she was sorry and if I ever wanted to talk, she would be open to that.

I didn't respond because I knew enough to know that I would mow her down with my words, if not my car, and with an act of divine grace, I withheld my response.

I hated her.

I looked for her everywhere.

Initially, I was obsessed with what she had, that I didn't. Youth, beauty and at one point the attention of my then husband.

I was furious at her.

It was hell.

Years passed and I still hurt and ached. I watched my marriage and the family I had invested in disintegrate before my eyes. I saw the devastation that my kids endured.

Time passed.

I knew deep down, if I ever did talk to her, I wanted it to be out of grace. Grace for both of us. An act of integrity. A choreographed response to what seemed like an atrocious injustice, not a rage-filled reaction.

I was doing a workshop on forgiveness and driving down the road without a thought of her, when all of a sudden, I knew I had forgiven her. It popped into my head. It's over. I thought, *I'm done with carrying her and her actions.*

It was never my plan to forgive her.

Nevertheless, by a divine act of mercy I had let go of my need to seek revenge and I had set her free.

I wanted to reach out. Not for her, but for me.

I had a session with my coach who had been through something similar. I told her that I wanted to reach out and have a conversation with her. My coach asked me lots of questions, checking to see if I was free from the deeply triggered emotions from that painful part of my life. My coach didn't want the conversation to trigger some unfinished business and have me come unhinged in Starbucks where we had arranged to meet.

So, we carefully planned the conversation and what I would say. Then, I reached out to her.

I called the number that was included in the email years before. I got a voice message. I was shaking and left a message. I said who I was and for her to call me back. Even to hear her recorded voice made me choke up. This was the voice of the "one," the one that had hurt me so deeply.

She texted back and asked what this was regarding and why I would like to meet, in order to be prepared.

I told her I was following up from her email, I intended no harm and I wanted to talk. We agreed to meet in a few days and picked a location.

I showed up 30 minutes early. My all-out pleading prayer was, "May I keep breathing, speak clearly and not have a melt-down." Asking not to cry would take more than a miracle, but to avoid a snotty, full-on bawl fest, felt like a reasonable request.

My heart was beating so fast. I told no one what I was doing. I wanted no one's opinion. I had worked it out with my coach and my God and that was enough.

I was shaking when she arrived. I knew her beauty and her youth, she was 15 years my junior. Do we need to mention the wrinkles I'd accumulated since this mess had started to unravel?

I said her name to get her attention as she walked by me. She sat down.

I held my cup of coffee so she wouldn't see my hands shaking and how unsettled I was.

Then, I said my rehearsed lines.

"Thank you for agreeing to meet me, that takes a lot of courage. I am going to speak first, and I ask that you not say anything until I am done."

She nodded.

I continued, "First of all, I wanted to tell you that what happened between you and my ex-husband was extremely devastating for myself and my children and it contributed to ending our marriage. Our family will never be the same. I also want to tell you that I am moving forward and, as a part of that, I have forgiven you and wanted you to know."

I had said my piece and made some peace too.

She told me that if she could say sorry a thousand times and go back and do things differently, she would. Which was appreciated but not needed.

As I sat across from her, I was not intimidated by her or her looks. I thought, *this is what beauty is-to be strong and courageous, to enter terrifying situations and do what feels right, for both of us.*

I did not have to do this and neither did she.

Forgiveness doesn't have easy steps. There's no five-point formula that gets you there in six months or less. It's also OK to not forgive. It's a choice.

For me, it was an act of grace, not all orchestrated by me. I did do A LOT of work to get there, however.

I wanted to live, and I wanted to live fully. I'd spent enough time wanting to die. I had to push through the rubble and create a life on the other side.

I had done the work. My work. I had to do the heavy lifting of working through what felt like a full-on disaster. She could not mend a shattered heart. She could not make amends to me or my kids.

Forgiveness is to stop carrying around the burden of what hurt you. It is to lay that down. I couldn't carry her any longer.

It's accepting that I would not seek revenge. Knowing there was nothing anyone could do to fix what had been destroyed.

I worked through the pain, with divine love, a therapist, a coach, daily reflections and journaling and I focused on me. If not for that, I would have stuck with plotting revenge day after day, formulating a plan to poison someone and in the meantime, the poison would have been eating me from the inside out.

I did the work, not because of some great strength, but because the pain of staying stuck was too intense so I kept going. One sloggy step at a time.

I sat across from her for what ended up being a 30-minute conversation. When we walked to my car, I told her I HAD thought that if I ever saw her, I would run her over, and that I was glad this is how things turned out. We chuckled (perhaps her more awkwardly than me), hugged and wished each other well.

That was it.

As I walked away from her, I felt joy.

There was a glimmer of joy in setting myself free. There was surprising joy in doing what I felt was right for me.

Forgiveness doesn't mean forgetting. There are parts of me that still get triggered when I feel I can't trust something or someone. I can still cry when I talk about that season of my life and even that day. But it's not the same. I don't carry that load like I used to.

My freedom is in forgiveness. I am not carrying the weight of revenge anymore. I have surrendered to the reality of my life; I have looked at it from all angles and I have set myself free.

Curious about exploring the 'F' word? It might be worth it.

Reflections

Are you carrying a burden and wondering if forgiveness might help?

What hurt you?

What would help to allow you to set aside the need for revenge and set yourself free?

What would you like to do as an act if integrity to bring some closure to this? (Get support if needed. I'm here if you need help.)

Chapter 52 (P/M)

"The Burn If I Die" Box

DO NOT OPEN THIS BOX

I had a box like that.

I thought I had a great marriage, and I knew we had a great family. Five days before I found out my husband of 16 years was having an affair; I told my friend that I still got butterflies when I thought of him. She told me we were one of only a few couples that she admired because it was clear we shared something special. Clearly not.

When I found out he was involved with someone else, I was committed to working things out. We were going to work through this. We were going to be one of those Armageddon rebuilding success stories.

That didn't happen.

I was absolutely devastated as I saw our marriage erode and our family fall apart.

Journaling is always something I have done, especially when I'm going through hard times. Writing gets out some of what's festering and hurting my soul. I have journaled every day for ten years. The good, the bad and the ugly. The very ugly.

It's like melted chocolate (well, any form of chocolate) for me. It's my way home.

There were things that I recorded with great detail about that time. I wrote down conversations and other things that came to the surface and, eventually, I wrote about the ugliness of the divorce process. It was all meticulously recorded in horrific detail.

The process helped me move through what had become a living hell.

I wanted someone, something, to bear witness to the absolute torture of feeling unloved and discarded. No one knew the extent of my heartbreak like my journals. No one knew the intensity of the feeling like I was slowly dying.

I needed a witness. Who would remember how I had struggled? How do you get up every morning and do normal things and feel absolutely decimated on the inside?

I had sleepless nights and days without eating. I had to go to work and pray I didn't spring a leak and have a flat-out nervous breakdown in front of a room of strangers.

It was by far the most excruciating thing I have ever been through. I felt like I was drowning most of the time. I did things I'm ashamed of like screaming at my husband in front of the kids. I was such a mess at times.

These journals recorded my life, my shame, and my devastation.

They were my anchor.

I needed them.

The events went on for a couple years. The unravelling was so intense and so unbearable. I thought of ending my life on several occasions.

The only thing that kept me alive was my kids, dear friends, my faith, and those words recorded, unedited in those journals.

It's been a decade since that all happened. And I never wanted my kids to read the words held on the pages, so I taped the journals up in a box. Then, I wrote a note and taped it to the top that clearly said, "Burn the box if I die".

The box was hidden under my stairs.

One day I knew it was time to throw out the box. It came to me while I was half asleep. I often am gently persuaded, with an intuitive nudge, at that time between wake and sleep, so that I know it's not my idea. Like a divine nudge.

I could never let the words written in hell be made public. What needs to be remembered always will be. I have a story that will not be put under the carpet, but the details will be left behind.

I threw the box in the garbage. I never opened the box or burnt it or shredded the pages. I didn't want to spend extra time with the contents of the box. The person who wrote those pages is not me anymore. Not who I am now at least. She's part of me and part of my story, but I am not her.

I threw out the box, said a little prayer of gratitude for how far I've come, for the grace that led me here and I recognized the grit that got me through. I cried. I'm sad that someone had to endure all of that.

Now I am also free.

I laid that burden in the bottom of a garbage can. I left it behind so I can make even more space for me and honour the healing and wholeness that came from what felt like a catastrophe. I feel lighter and I feel blessed. I feel like it was an act of forgiveness-letting go of the record.

There is joy in release.

Is there a *burn if I die* box hiding under the stairs of your life?

You may never throw your box away, that's OK. Follow your nudges.

Reflections

Is there anything in the meantime that you want to let go of?

Is there anything that if you got rid of it you would feel set free?

What's one step you can take to set yourself free?

Chapter 53 (M)

Got an Umbrella?

I hate rain-ruins the hair, wrecks the shoes… it's not my thing. I bought an umbrella a couple of years ago from the kid's section of Walmart, to spark some joy on a rainy day. It has flowers and butterflies on it to protect myself from the elements and the foul mood that rain brings me.

Life had been feeling stormy and yet I felt like I have been moving through its events protected somehow.

By an umbrella of grace.

As I reflected on a really tough, unforgettable week I'd had, I realized that the less one fights situations that are not controllable and surrenders to what is, the burden oddly becomes lighter.

A belief like that can have a huge impact on how one views the world and how one interacts within that world.

I hold strongly to the belief that nothing is a mistake and that you'll never be given more than you can handle. I trust that.

I rest my life in that.

You may feel overwhelmed, stretched, squished, but you won't be snuffed out.

You will have whatever you need when you need it, often not much before you need it and so often in what feels like the nick of time. That's grace to me

Here's my wee life equation-the *essence* of my umbrella; my protection:

Surrender + Trust = Grace

Grace is defined as undeserved favour-like the gift of finding an umbrella on a rainy day.

The forecast at that time as I headed into a regular week, was *clear skies*, looking so balanced and filled with clients and a variety of events. It was going to be great and it was, just way different than I expected.

Monday, I got a text that my 75-year-old dad had a very bad headache. He went to the doctor and was rushed to the hospital by ambulance.

Tuesday morning, I woke up to the text that they saw metastasized brain cancer on a scan.

Later that evening, I got a text from my son who also had a brain tumour and was awaiting surgery in a couple of months after he completed high school. He told me he was having really terrible shooting pain in his head when he lifted things at work. It was something that his surgeon had said to watch out for and was a sign that his brain surgery might need to be moved up.

I started to feel overwhelmed. I decided to wait and see if my son's symptoms would go away.

Wednesday came and the diagnosis was in. My dad had the most aggressive form of brain cancer. It was a terminal diagnosis. We needed a family meeting to decide on treatment options. I finished my morning of work and drove for three hours to be with my family.

My son's headache was dull that morning so I felt that I could get away for the night.

It was not a drizzle of stress; it was heavy downpour. I called a friend to talk about the stress, yet I felt an odd peace.

It felt like there was an umbrella over me in a storm.

I was still getting wet, just not as bad as expected by the appearance of the circumstances in this storm.

I get that people get cancer and that my son's brain tumours run in our family. I know those two realities, but to be struggling with those two realities in the same week seemed crazy to me. Insane really.

My mind returned to my belief. My truth.

Leona, you are not given more than you can handle.

I felt like I was moving under an umbrella of grace made up of surrender and trust.

The week was hard, beautiful, and rich.

It seemed like it was pouring all around me and my job was to hold fast to the umbrella and not rush ahead into the storm. I had to remain where I was, where my feet were, in every moment.

The important thing about an umbrella is to stay underneath it. If you run, it can't keep you dry. I really focused on being present.

What if you believed that whatever you are facing was not a mistake? That you have exactly what you need for whatever lies in your path?

How would that change things?

Can you surrender to what's out of your control? What is your umbrella in those times called? Maybe it's truth or grit or love.

Whatever it is, know that it's there for you to provide a wee bit of shelter in a storm.

There's an umbrella here for you too...

Reflections

What are the messages that go through your head when you feel very overwhelmed?

When you look back at hard times do you see a glimpse of an umbrella in your life in those times?

Taking what you have experienced, is there a statement that helps you hold steadier in the stormy weather that life sometimes throws your way?

Hold onto that statement when times are tough. Or use mine-you will always have what you need when you need it. Or you'll never have more than you can handle.

How might this set of beliefs provide a wee buffer for the storms that rage around you?

Chapter 54 (M)

Um…

Um… Um…

I was a guest on a podcast, and I was so shocked at how often how I said *um*.

I was mortified by how I spoke. Why was I like that? Did I always pepper every conversation with a million ums? (Probably). I was mortified to even think about that and how I must sound to people who have to listen to me. UGH. So, I made some pretty big decisions based on this horrifying experience.

I decided I would never be doing another podcast, speak in public or run workshops. Basically, a big part of my livelihood I would throw out the window. I would cancel my upcoming speaking engagements and move on with my life from the comfort of my wee home office and not expose myself to the humiliation of being heard speaking aloud ever again.

Isn't that how a flaw makes us feel? Like hiding? Like playing small.

I also hadn't written a blog in a while and when I finally did, I received some comments about how my blogs had improved.

What I took from that comment was that I had been a horrible writer prior to that. How shameful to think that I had been writing blogs for a few years and they were absolute crap (that was the story I made up based on the comment).

Well the proverbial writing was on the wall-STOP WRITING Leona!! I was worried about how bad my writing must have been prior to that so I stopped writing all together. No speaking or writing for Leona. Stay safe. No more exposure for this girl. Nope. No way.

AVOID ALL THE VULNERABILITIES!

I convinced myself that I could not go back to writing the fluff that my blogs must be filled with and would keep my writing for my journal. Full on fluff fest there.

Except…I don't blog because I think I'm a great blogger and I don't speak because I think I am a great speaker (although I have slowed down and don't say um nearly as much ;). I talk and write to let people know we're in this muck of life together. That we're all flawed and that saying "um" and writing less than perfectly is showing up anyway.

My coach asked me once about being a runner. I said, emphatically, "I AM NOT A RUNNER."

"Oh," she said. "I thought you said you ran."

I laughed and said, "I do, but I'm not a runner."

The truth was I ran about four times per week at that time and I had been running for 5 years at least that often. Because it was challenging (OK freaking hard) to run I didn't consider myself a runner. I just ran and panted and felt like dying most days.

I wanted to avoid the vulnerability of someone looking at me and thinking, *that's hardly running. You can't call yourself a runner.* Exactly! I couldn't agree more!

I wanted to, and still want to, avoid that icky feeling of being vulnerable. I don't want to expose myself to the world unless I'm a great writer, a great runner, and an exceptional speaker. Perfectionism can be my shield. Bring on all the shields in fact! ;)

I bet you don't like exposure either. Vulnerability, at its worst, feels like walking around in a trench coat, flashing people. That's full-frontal exposure. I DO NOT LIKE THAT AND I WANT TO AVOID THAT! I bet you do too (not just me flashing you, clearly, but feeling that exposed in any area of your life).

We don't have to be perfect to be seen and show up. The goodness comes in the showing up; and only in continuing to choose courage over the comfort we so crave, will our craft be truly mastered.

I write, I do presentations and I facilitate workshops and if I didn't, I wouldn't be doing what I believe I'm meant to do. I would be soooo outside of integrity encouraging you to bring your magic into the world, while still hiding myself.

I do hope to be even more mindful and ditch more of the *ums* by the time I deliver my first TED Talk. I do hope I've deepened and honed my writing craft since you are reading this book and you are in deep.

My deepest desire is not that you'll be impressed with my writing but, if nothing else, you'll think:

If Leona's doing her thing, I can too. YES, YOU CAN!!!!

Know that I'm running alongside you and cheering on your bravery. I won't settle for playing it safe and, um, I hope you won't either. Whatever you have a burning desire to bring to the world. BRING IT!! Maybe even you're just curious about something, please pursue it. That's where joy lives and is waiting for you.

Where are you hiding?

Reflections

What would you love to pursue if you weren't afraid of what people would think?

What would it be like for you to pursue that?

What's one thing you will do to give yourself permission to pursue that which you have been hiding?

Chapter 55 (A)

Nothing Will Ever Change

I think most of us would like to change something. If we want to create a change that sticks, we have to start on the inside. On ourselves.

We fundamentally change our outer worlds, working from the inside out. I think you probably are picking up on this as you move through this book.

Think of the last time you made a new year's resolution. How well did you stick to it? How long did the intended change last?

I'm guessing not as long as you may have liked. If you're reading this on a treadmill right now, things may have worked out well for you. ;)

We try new things and commit to change, but so often we don't make long-term changes because we have literally only scratched the surface of why we want to do what we're doing.

I've already given you some tools to move deeper to understand what's going on behind the scenes.

Once you've created some stillness, notice your brain clutter. Then you can start to close some open tabs in your brain and focus on what you want in your life.

One of the reasons that long-term change doesn't happen, or stick, is because it's not attached to much. What deliciousness would it give you to see an action item be implemented in five years?

Things get juiced up.

You need to get clear on your values. Here they are again. They show up everywhere when we are creating the life we really want. The change you long for may be so much deeper than weight loss, but we'll look at that because a common goal and can give us the wisdom we need.

I am healthy, I can move and that's such a gift! I've stuck to my commitment to being healthy for 15 years because of my values. I want to honour the gift of my life lived out in this body of mine so I think, *what will honour this body daily?* My value of honour keeps my commitment a top priority. That's a joy spot for me.

I try to move and eat healthy daily, because of honour. I've been super blessed to have an amazing body, not the kind that I would put on a poster next to a super model, but it's amazing, nonetheless. It moves (even when I've had awful pain), it digests food, it rests, it holds someone's hand. You get the idea.

Maybe you want to feel better in your skin, maybe you want to have more energy. Sink into that. Feel what it was like the last time you felt like that. Go way back to when you were a rock star kiddo doing cartwheels on your front lawn. Wasn't that awesome?!

Do you remember that feeling? Was it freedom? Play? Lightness? How will making this desired change help you feel that desired feeling? Then start taking some wee steps and plan to move ahead. It's all held together with the foundation of the values you want to honour and the feels you want to feel.

This is where the yum factor is upped BIG time and you start to feel great and motivated.

I'll let you in on a wee secret, one change leads to another and to another and so on and so on and you'll find yourself living a life you never thought was possible.

Another key to making change stick is to start SMALL.

Take super small steps in the direction of the change that you want.

Here's why. When we feel successful our brain produces dopamine, a wee hormone that rewards our brain and makes us feel good. It's a spark of joy. Like a joy spot in your brain, hello goodness!!

When the success is easy, the dopamine comes easy and our brain LOVES that reward, so it gets excited to get more of it.

This could look like wanting to write a blog. Make it a daily habit for daily dopamine hits. Make your goal small. Commit to writing a sentence a day or writing for three minutes.

Studies show that people that start this small stick with the habit and build on it as they go along and have a much greater chance of sticking with the change that they are trying to make. How awesome is that?!

Visualize what you want to achieve. We use 90 per cent of the same brain power when we are doing something, as we do when we visualize it. So, visualize spending time writing. Visualize how amazing it will feel when you're done your blog; feel those feelings, that joy. That will also increase the likelihood that you will continue.

Fun random fact: basketball players who practiced their free throws and those who visualized the same practice both had a 23 per cent increase in accuracy. Can't sleep tonight? Visualize something awesome that you want to achieve and do something super awesome with your restless brain.

Reflections

What's something that you would like to change in your life?

Is there a list?

Write that out and commit to daily, very small practices. Set a reminder to do it.

If you want to walk more, set a reminder to walk to the end of the street. That's it. Having trouble with that? Set a reminder to just put on your shoes.

Start soooo small and watch your success build!

Chapter 56 (A)

Make Them Juicy

I think you knew there would be a chapter on goal setting. It's the foundation of any good business plan and we are in the joy creating business.

For many of us, we have some ideas of what we want, but to set specific goals and then actually achieve them is not easy to do. Accomplishment does give us joy.

One of the most effective ways to set some of the juiciest goals is to look at your core values, those "must haves" in your life.

I know you've heard so much about values, soooo much, but they are the KEY to fulfillment, resilience, and JOY.

Goal setting isn't a favourite for many of us because we know our follow-through in the past may have been lacking. In fact, with goal setting comes the dreaded streeeetch and the gremlins running around in our heads saying, "Are you kidding me-you're going to do what?!"

People achieve tremendous success (and delight) in using their values to light the way. For example, look at your values:

Connection, Integrity, Joy, Passion (always moving forward) and Honour.

Take each one and look at how you can honour those more fully in your life.

Ask yourself, "What's one thing that I could do to take those values to the next level?"

Let's explore Connection.

Ask yourself, "What do I want to be deeply connected to in my life?" Partner, children, team, higher self…

"What could I do to increase those connections?"

"How could I make it even more tangible by creating a weekly or daily habit?"

Perhaps the goal around this value becomes: Sunday meal with kids, daily meditation, connect with member on the team for 15 minutes a week…

Set reminders to make sure this happens, and a habit is formed.

To take this to the next level, develop some accountability around those goals. For instance, let others know about them and ask for some help in making sure the goals are implemented and tweaked as needed to keep you in this delicious new groove, just like we talked about in another chapter.

Keep these goals front and centre. Make a vision board that has pictures that represent what you want to achieve. Or make a list of your goals and put it somewhere where you see it often. I have a friend that keeps this in her bathroom, so she sees it every time she sits down. I love that!

The draw is that when we are living in line with our values and honouring them in very intentional ways, we're jazzed up. We feel great. We find our flow and our energy is high (you may even hear a few angels sing - can you hear them already? ;))

Reflections

100 things

Grab a pen and paper and write for 20 minutes (set a timer) without stopping and write down 100 things you want to be, do, and achieve in this lifetime. (Have a friend do it too. It's so inspiring!)

You don't have to do all of these. The point is to go back over them and see if there are some that spark joy for you. Keep those front and center and set some goals around those joy spots.

Because you weren't able to stop writing, you may notice that there are themes which are repetitive. Take those items and see what steps you can start with to move towards those joy spots. Your life is richer already for having done this!

Chapter 57 (A/M)

Your Word

I adore people who set hard ass goals and create some strong strategic objectives and check them out at least quarterly. I LOVE THOSE people.

They are my people; these disciplined, ritualistic, hard working AWESOME PEOPLE!

I consider them my tribe. I know them. I hope we share DNA.

But I feel like I've had discipline and worked hard and played by a whole bunch of rules for pretty much my entire life. I need to do things differently and be a wee less rigid so I can let more joy sneak in. ;)

I get up at a certain time everyday-early. Doesn't matter if I slept crappy, I am up. No excuses. Can you hear the drill sergeant that lives in my head? I Meditate. Pray. Journal. Move. Wooooork. Wish I had got more done. Wee caveat here, I'm not made of steel, and I need an almost daily nap before moving into my evening routine. I am the queen of routine.

Start again the next day.

For some reason, I'm being drawn, OK pushed, in a different direction.

I feel half dead a lot of days and the rituals that I have set do help get me through, but I need something else. Don't get me wrong, I LOVE my work. Love my work. Coaching is my lifeblood. I am so grateful for it, but I am wound up TIGHT.

In my mind, I feel relaxed. However, my body, my physiotherapist and my other village of people helping me find wellness know differently.

I am intentionally trying to relax more, move slowly and do deep stretching to help those creaky muscles. Thank goodness for JoySocks, as I spend lots of time laying with my bum up against the wall, looking at my socked feet on the wall above me. It's the small mercies that get us all through. That is one of mine.

So, I'm reluctantly responding to the draaaaag of my achy body to tell me to relax more, with the tell-tale metaphorical road rash on my body as I RESIST, as I move against my will, in a different direction.

Where am I moving?

I move toward grace.

That's my word for the year. OK, the rest of my life. On my birthday, I always ask for my word for the year, and this year the first word that popped into my head was grace. I love that word (thank goodness!) I've had audacious as my word before and I am not up for that right now. Although this whole *relax more* thing does feel slightly audacious for this one.

Grace reminds me of being held and being cherished, no matter who I am or what I do. It's like being gripped in King Kong's hands and being carried from one thing to the other, minus the terrifying gorilla part.

I don't have to try so hard, worry so much or figure out so much.

There are less rules, there is less stress, and there is more all out goodness.

A couple of months into my year of grace, I've got new great clients sans marketing, beautiful existing ones are continuing to allow me to journey alongside them, and I have new opportunities for my business and life that I am very excited about. That is grace to me.

In my newly carved out space, I have found more meaning in being creative, and for me that's mostly writing. Words come more easily and less restrained when you realize how finite life and health are. I know I should know this already, but this chronic pain bump in the road has made it even more clear. You know I'm a slow learner.

I worry less about my writing and just write.

Creating feels good regardless of what it looks or reads like.

I've let go of everyone liking what I produce. My role is to write, as it brings meaning to life's madness for me. Like coaching, I don't feel uncomfortable when I'm doing it. I am in the zone and feel flow. It brings peace to me and helps me find my way back to grace.

I know there's a word or phrase for you that would support you. What is it?

Reflections

What's your word?

Is there an image that helps you stay grounded in that word?

What will you do every day to live more inline with your word?

Chapter 58 (P)

Peeking Over the Fence

Is the grass really greener on the other side?

Have you ever peeked over the fence to see?

Is the grass thick and lush?

What's going on over there?

I spoke with a friend and things in her business seemed to be falling into place with such ease. She has new clients and a new office space. Everything seems to come so easy to her.

I peered over my fence to look at her grass.

Damn, her grass is pretty green. It looks amazing in fact!

While I was happy for her, I found myself looking at the grass on my side of that metaphorical fence. Things didn't seem nearly as green if it was at all green. Dammit, I'm watering, fertilizing, and mulching too, yet I've noticed some bald patches that could use some more work.

Then I heard a wee whisper while my head was peaking over the fence…

"Comparison is the thief of joy."

Ya, whatever.

I know that, but how do we keep from comparing ourselves to others? I know that drinking too much coffee isn't good for me either, but occasionally I have too many cups. How do we stop doing what we know isn't good for us?

Some things come to mind that'll help us focus on our own "yards".

Recognize your own story about the situation.

Things seem easy on the other side, but the truth lies in between. The stories we make up can hijack us in the meantime. I made up that everything was easy for her, but I don't know what actually keeps this friend awake at night. I don't know for sure that all is easy on her side of the fence, like it looks.

One thing that has helped to stop comparison is to genuinely celebrate another person's successes. Life is generous, not scarce-there's enough goodness for all of us. ALL of us!

Realize there is nothing to compare, really. We all have different lives, we're here to serve different purposes and comparing them takes away your own sense of purpose and gumption.

Do we need to compare apples to oranges? If we get to pick, I always go mango. My fave. Exotic and juicy. Sorry, I digress.

No, they're all delicious in their own way. So, while you think you're comparing your 'grass' to another's, it's so vastly more complicated than what we see. Trust your own deliciousness.

Be grateful for what you do have. Get out of comparison and focus on what you have to be grateful for. There is always something to be thankful for.

Keep moving forward, put on some blinders if you need to, don't look to the right or the left, just take the next step on your own journey. Stop looking over the fence. STOP. Stay in your lane.

Do something that lights you up and sparks joy for you. When life is a little dull, everything else looks shiny and sparkly compared to what you have going on.

Focus on cultivating joy in your yard. Plant yourself a garden full of joy. Metaphorically speaking or literally. You do you.

What sparks joy for you?

What feels meaningful and delicious?

What makes your heart sing? Do more of that.

KNOW deeply that you were meant to serve a distinct purpose, or multi purposes on the planet, and while the path may not always be clear or easy, you have a role to serve in your time here.

Purpose doesn't mean one thing. It means being more of you, doing more of what makes you feel amazing and lose track of time.

If you don't know what feels purposeful or meaningful, I've got you and I've so been there. Reach out. I can help. In the meantime, think about what you're curious about, and move in that direction.

Start small. Heck, blow your hair back with some big bold moves! Whatever you do, DO something!

You're here to make a difference. Spend time exploring that, the sweet intersection of your skills, passion, and experience. That's your joy spot!

The more time you spend in that sweet joy spot the less time you will have to peek over any fences.

Your *grass* is yours and yours alone, and it is as unique as you are. Lean into that lushness. You guessed it-that's joy!

Reflections

What situations make you look over the fence into other people's yards?

What stressors cause you to compare yourself to others?

What can you focus on, in your own yard, that will create more joy and meaning so you'll be less likely to compare?

When you cultivate more meaning and joy in your life you won't have the need or energy to compare yourself to others.

Feel some joy gurgling up?

Chapter 59 (A/M/E)

Pssst...It Wants You as Much as You Want It

Whether it's your passion, something you've had an idea about doing or exploring but keep putting it off, or something you don't dive into it as passionately as you want, here's the truth.

It wants you too.

Are you being pursued?

I read Elizabeth Gilbert's book *Big Magic*, and it made amazing magical sense. (If you have not read it, go buy it, read it, lick the pages, and cook it up for breakfast, because it will change your world. It changed mine.)

Elizabeth (I call all people, even ones that I don't know, by their first names) speaks about creativity pursuing us as much as we want to pursue it. When we get an idea, we should go for it; we should dive in, not for the purpose of fame or fortune, but simply because it came to us for a reason.

Your creative project may not make you money, win you awards, or make the bestseller list, but it captures you. Time doesn't matter. If you could get paid for it, it would be the first and last job that you would ever apply for. That's pure yum-a real live whopping joy spot.

I am sitting here madly writing this book. I have no idea where this will end up. I do hope more than just you and my honey will read it (fingers crossed, maybe my kids). I want people to have lives that are filled with meaning and huge spots of joy that splatter them like a well tossed water balloon in the face (gently of course) when they least expect it and most need it.

If this book could help, I'd be over the moon happy. If this book helps encourage you to pursue something that you've always wanted to pursue or have been curious about, then that would be amazeballs.

SO, pursue what you're interested in. DO not, in this case, begin with the end in mind. Just start. I started JoySocks by giving away some fun socks to people. Then, following my son's hospitalization, I decided to send a simple email to the Ronald McDonald house asking if they wanted some fun socks. Eventually, JoySocks evolved to over 10,000 socks having been given away to people who could use a smile. I had no idea this would happen.

Our purpose and our joy spots show their bright shiny heads in our creative endeavours. If you've got your hands on your hips right now, about to say that you're "not one of those" join the club. I was one of you.

Just listen.

We are ALL creative. It just shows up in different ways. We know we've found that when we find the feeling of flow.

Flow means engagement. It means when we lose track of time but are still miraculously present. Even coffee and wine start to matter less. (OK perhaps that's just me.)

For some that might be painting, developing new software, reorganizing closets, or taking photos. I love starting new companies and diving into new business initiatives. The angels sing every time. Whether it's with a client or working in one of my own companies, when I'm being creative, it feels like bliss-filled heaven.

Be curious. Make space for creativity like we've talked about before. Don't settle.

Passion begets passion, and you may light a fire in your life that won't be easily contained. That will be amazing!!

If passion isn't even in your vocabulary and if you're worn out just thinking about it, start with what you're mildly curious about, even if that just shows up as having more than one thought about something in particular. It may be as simple as putting your bare feet in the dirt to see what it feels like. Start there.

There's a wee bit of magic to be sprinkled on this passion-filled cupcake that you're creating and taking a bite out of. You may just discover that, as you pursue something, you're excited about, it will pursue you. Doors will open, you'll meet people who are like minded and opportunities will become available. Just know that a certain amount of ease and joy will start to bubble up and that you've created that joy. Look at you go.

"Create whatever causes a revolution in your heart. The rest of it will take care of itself." (Elizabeth Gilbert, *Big Magic*)

I want a revolution in my heart. I want to start a revolution in your heart too.

Reflections

What are you curious about?

What have you thought about a couple times this week already?

What would you love to explore more of?

What will you do to pursue more of what you're curious about?

Chapter 60 (M)

Let's Define It

Success to me means doing what I love, being with the people I love, and helping others uncover their truth and find more joy.

I want to honour all I have been given and help you do the same so we can all screech across the finish line of this life at a ripe old age (cognitively intact and diaper free, if I am to get specific).

Life doesn't come with many guarantees, so it is important that we define what makes life rich and meaningful.

What DOES success mean to you?

What do you want to be, have, and do in the next 50 years?

How do you measure wealth?

Is it by the money in your bank account?

How big your retirement fund is?

How much revenue your business is generating?

Is it about having more time?

How many pairs of goofy socks you have? (OK maybe that's just me-I have A LOT!)

You have been given this one wildly precious life-what will you do with it?

What will you invest in it to get the greatest returns?

What is your heart calling you to do?

Please, please…make this life matter.

Set aside "busy."

Sluff off "have to."

Follow the path toward what makes you feel opulently wealthy.

One of the most important measures of wealth for me is:

TIME

My dad, after only being sick for a few days, was diagnosed with one of the most aggressive forms of brain cancer that, with very few exceptions, is always fatal within 12 months. I mentioned this already.

I went to see him and listened to what the doctor said about treatment and outcomes. Dad responded by saying he wanted aggressive treatment so he could have more of what was most important:

TIME.

It was one of the most moving and powerful experiences to hear my dad, who had just received horrific news, speak with gratitude about his blessed life, and with the strength and determination to make his remaining days really matter.

He talked about how grateful he was for his life, loving my mom for her time on earth and his current wife of over 20 years. His life was not easy. He was an immigrant with a grade 8 education. He ran his own business, and things were often tight. Part of the reason money was often tight was that he was busy giving away his services and never sending invoices. He was so grateful for the richness of his life. He felt he had spent his life using the time he was given well. That time and the way he used it made him feel rich.

His life felt SO full and so meaningful. I want that for me when the time comes. I desperately want that for you.

Would you pursue that? It will be the BEST thing you ever invest in. I promise you and, in the meantime, as you pursue that, you will inspire others to do the same, and so on and so on and so on.

DO this with relentless intent.

Seeing my dad, knowing his days were numbered and being reminded that mine are too, I am constantly making changes, investing in some different things; things that bring me life and, hopefully, a fuller life to others too.

Fill your life with the riches that align with how you define success, make you feel extravagantly wealthy and, while you're doing that, purge the things that take away from that. Be intentional with your one magical life.

Reflections

Create a list of what you want this life to be filled with in order to be successful.

What will really matter to you in the end? What's your legacy?

How do you measure wealth?

What do you need to start investing wisely in?

Write your own obituary or eulogy if you haven't yet and see what that says about how you define success.

Chapter 61 (A)

Don't Settle

Don't Settle, DON'T SETTLE, DON'T SETTLE!!!

That is it. That is all.

I've been thinking of all the amazing things that I have received in my life, some I've worked for, while others seem to have been dropped from above-pure, blissful gifts that I'd dreamt of, but never thought I would get to experience.

Some include; starting and maintaining three companies, raising three lovely, resilient and amazing kiddos, having a delicious partner, owning my own home, having a new car (it's a wee red car that I call the Joy ride, which I bought to honour my disappeared pancreatic tumour). And I've exceeded the life expectancy of a woman with my condition; so many goodnesses. The list is long and that's just a start.

What this made me realize was that, at many times in my life I've thought, this is good enough, you're not going to do any better. I wanted to settle.

In those times I heard a little voice nudge me to leave the *good* behind and hold out for the *great*.

I used to ignore it, but recently I've been taking its sage advice.

I'm willing to bet you've experienced this too.

For instance, it could be having a good job and wanting something different; and so, with a whole bunch of courage, you've chosen to leave.

Perhaps it's leaving some security and even some money behind, in order to move toward something that feeds your soul-maybe it's a new job, career, or even starting your own business.

Maybe it's leaving a mediocre relationship because it's costing you more than you're getting in return.

It could be speaking up in a tough situation.

You know what I'm talking about.

Where are you settling, right now, in your own life?

Hear the nudge?

Calling you into greatness.

Making the choice to not settle takes boat loads of courage, but it is soooo worth it.

You've got everything you need to hold out and create a life filled with a whole bucket of greatness.

Don't settle for good…not for one more second. Go for great!

Fill your boots with courage and start stepping towards what your heart longs for and you deserve.

You'll be surprised what awaits you, I promise.

Reflections

What's nudging you?

What idea would you love to make a reality?

What's your call to greatness?

What would you LOVE to pursue?

What would you like to fill your life with that would bring you the most joy?

What will you do, starting right now, to make your life richer?

What would make your life feel more meaningful?

What else will you do with this one delicious life?

What would bring you more joy?

Chapter 62 (M/A)

What Mark Will You Leave?

What's your legacy? What are you going to leave behind? How are you making your *mark* on the world?

In the summer of 1992, my beloved momma died, and I experienced one of the greatest losses of my life.

I have now been longer without her than I had been with her. I often reflect on what she had taught me in the time that she blessed me with her presence.

I posted a picture of her on Facebook and was astounded by the comments of people who barely had contact with her over the years. These people told me what an amazing person she was and what impact she had had on them in a short period of time.

My mom, without knowing it, left an amazing legacy.

She left a legacy of joy, love, generosity, and trust.

Anyone who knew her came face-to-face with her joy. She was simple and unassuming, quick to smile, and she enjoyed the sweet things in life that so many others overlooked. She hadn't had an easy life. She had her first brain tumor at age 24. She had been told she only had a 10 per cent chance of survival because of its location but survive she did. Thrive she did (sorry little yodaness here). She was always cheerful and smiling-always living life with her cup "half full." OK, more like overflowing.

She went on to really live life to the fullest. She had 10 more brain surgeries over the next 25 years. You wouldn't have known of her suffering, she never talked about it, but focused on how grateful she was to be alive, and raising her kids.

She showered those near her with love.

She never nagged us about messy rooms or the crazy house that we created or the work it took to cook our meals and do our laundry. Her kids never had to help with any chores. (Though I'm not suggesting that needs to part of the legacy you may want to leave. :)

My mom seemed to relish her time with us every day and was thrilled to be around to raise us. She delighted in us, bathing us in love. I learned true love from her.

She cared nothing of worldly wealth. In fact, some years she gave away 30 per cent of the family's earnings to charity, which meant our family lived below the poverty line. We had no idea. We were always fed and so deeply cherished. Life was so good.

I loved her and feel sad for her shortened life of 49 years, and the fact that my kids never got to know her. I also celebrate her.

I want to create a legacy like hers. (Mine, however, includes household chores for my kidlets. :)

I want to leave a *mark*.

When I was diagnosed with my first two brain tumours, it reminded me of her legacy, the condition I inherited from her. I struggled with this. I don't want these tumours.

If I'm to honour my mother and carry on her legacy, I have to be willing to accept the parts of her that aren't an easy pill to swallow. That means accepting the tough parts and being open to living a life rich in faith and trust, even when things are hard, like she did.

My mom, who seemingly knew nothing of how to create a legacy or worldly success, certainly had a massive impact.

The touch of her life will be felt for generations to come because she lived a full life, focused on blessing others, and that's what really matters in the end.

Focus today on having an impact on the lives of those you encounter, on being a blessing, on making a difference, on making your mark.

What will your mark be?

Please LIVE YOUR LEGACY. Fill the world with more joy, love and meaning like only you can.

Reflections

Start each day with the thought of the mark you want to leave, the impact you desire to have and the legacy you want to create.

What do you want to be remembered for?

What beautiful mark do you want to leave?

Commit each day to creating that legacy and leaving your magic sprinkled everywhere you go.

You're a delicious treat, here for a glorious reason. Stamp that truth on this earth and leave your mark everywhere.

We need your magic.

Epilogue

Beloved reader my hope as you moved through this book you felt more meaning, purpose, and perhaps greater courage to live a life that you are actively designing to be filled with joy. My desire is that in the pages of this book you found more delicious joy spots that you hadn't noticed before.

There are no names in this book, and I did this because if you could see yourself on any of its pages and know a truer version of yourself through the stories, that was my deepest desire.

Know your truth more; know more joy.

I don't want our time together to end. Please continue your joy journey over at findingyourjoyspot.com. I've got some delicious treats waiting for you over there! You can download some extra goodies to keep the joy journey rolling.

In case you skipped the intro, you may have noticed that here was a letter by the title of each chapter which corresponded with one of the 5 scientifically proven components of flourishing and happiness (aka joy). They are:

P-Positive Emotions

E-Engagement

R-Relationships (healthy connection)

M-Meaning

A-Accomplishment

Focus on these 5 aspects of your life and the other nuggets of wisdom in this book and you will find more joy, I promise AND more meaning and more goodness. You may even live longer (there's some great science around that), perhaps I'll save that for the next book. In the meantime, go find your joy spots!!

About the Author

Leona deVinne is someone who needed three years of coaching to write her first blog, only later to be personally invited by Arianna Huffington to blog for the Huff Post, and now a book. Proof, my friends, that miracles do happen! Leona's mission is to help people find more joy by bringing their gifts and talents to the world. In her work as a professional coach, she is dedicated (ok maybe slightly obsessed, but in a nice way ;) with helping others live their best lives and supporting them as they take their ideas and make them a reality. She can not get enough of the goodness of others and the magic that they bring to the world. She loves nothing more than seeing others shine. She lives in Calgary, Canada with her most beloved husband, 3 of the best bio babies and 2 stepdaughters. Connect with Leona via Facebook (TheJoySpot/), Instagram (thejoyspot), her website (www.leonadevinne.com / www.findingyourjoyspot.com) and email leona@leonadevinne.com.

Acknowledgements

First of all, you, beloved reader, thank you for getting this far and holding this book in your hands and digesting its words. You can not even imagine the gratitude I have for you. Thank you!!! All the hugs and kisses to you. I have to thank my first coach, Shannon, who died in Jan 2016. She is the reason I started to write. Bless her for seeing that all things are possible for a broken woman that she supported back to life. My most amazing love, Rod, for loving all of me and my words. He's the simply the best, such a gift, and massive support. My most incredible and courageous kids, Sara, Leah, and Josh. These lambs have been through the fire and are my biggest blessings. My sister in law, my ex sister in law, actually, who we joke I got in the divorce, for being my best friend and one of my final editors on this book. My friend Fran who reads more books than anyone I know and was the first to take a peek and make the preliminary edits and did not tell me to trash the whole thing. My coach Laurie, who knows me and calls me on my stuff when I play small and has helped me play a much bigger game. Much thanks for my incredibly gifted brander and designer, Nikki at Fetching Finn. She is the magic behind the cover of this book and all my web design. Much thanks to Lea at Our Family Lines for pulling all of this together. It takes a village. Thanks also to coffee and wine, they have been faithful and true. And finally, the biggest heart full of gratitude and joy for the Love that surrounds us all and makes all things possible.

Sources

Brown, B. (2012). *Daring greatly: How the courage to be vulnerable transforms the way we live, love, parent, and lead.* Gotham Books.

Brown, B. (2015). *Rising Strong* (First edition.). Spiegel & Grau.

Brown, B. (2010). *The gifts of imperfection: Let go of who you think you're supposed to be and embrace who you are.* Hazelden.

Gilbert, E. (2015). *Big magic: Creative living beyond fear.* Riverhead Books.

Lerner, H. G. (2001). *The dance of connection: How to talk to someone when you're mad, hurt, scared, frustrated, insulted, betrayed, or desperate.* HarperCollins.

Louden, J. (2013). *The life organizer: A woman's guide to a mindful year.* New World Library.

McKeown, G. (2014). *Essentialism: The Disciplined Pursuit of Less.* Currency.

Northrup, Christiane, https://www.drnorthrup.com/

Rodgers, Richard, composer. Hammerstein, Oscar II, Lyricist "Do-Re-Mi"-The Sound of Music (1965)

Seligman, M. (2011). *Flourish: A visionary new understanding of Happiness and Well-being.* Free Press.

Wiseman, Teresa, (1996) Journal of Advanced Nursing 23,1162-1167 A concept analysis of empathy

Manufactured by Amazon.ca
Bolton, ON